CAMBRIDGE LIBRARY COLLECTION

Books of enduring scholarly value

British and Irish History, Nineteenth Century

This series comprises contemporary or near-contemporary accounts of the political, economic and social history of the British Isles during the nineteenth century. It includes material on international diplomacy and trade, labour relations and the women's movement, developments in education and social welfare, religious emancipation, the justice system, and special events including the Great Exhibition of 1851.

Guide to the Mount's Bay and the Land's End

President of the Royal College of Physicians from 1844 until his death, John Ayrton Paris (1785–1856) wrote chiefly on medical topics, yet he also devoted time to the study of science and natural history. He served as physician to the Penzance Dispensary between 1813 and 1817, during which time he helped to establish what became the Royal Geological Society of Cornwall. First published anonymously in 1816, and reissued here in the second edition of 1824, this work explores the landscapes and natural history of the western part of Cornwall. Presented as a series of 'excursions', the guide takes in locations such as St Michael's Mount and the Lizard, also covering the rich mining districts at Redruth and St Just, and discussing local customs, the Cornish language and the health-giving climate. Several of Paris's medical and biographical works are also reissued in this series, including his life of the Cornish chemist Sir Humphry Davy.

Cambridge University Press has long been a pioneer in the reissuing of out-of-print titles from its own backlist, producing digital reprints of books that are still sought after by scholars and students but could not be reprinted economically using traditional technology. The Cambridge Library Collection extends this activity to a wider range of books which are still of importance to researchers and professionals, either for the source material they contain, or as landmarks in the history of their academic discipline.

Drawing from the world-renowned collections in the Cambridge University Library and other partner libraries, and guided by the advice of experts in each subject area, Cambridge University Press is using state-of-the-art scanning machines in its own Printing House to capture the content of each book selected for inclusion. The files are processed to give a consistently clear, crisp image, and the books finished to the high quality standard for which the Press is recognised around the world. The latest print-on-demand technology ensures that the books will remain available indefinitely, and that orders for single or multiple copies can quickly be supplied.

The Cambridge Library Collection brings back to life books of enduring scholarly value (including out-of-copyright works originally issued by other publishers) across a wide range of disciplines in the humanities and social sciences and in science and technology.

Guide to the Mount's Bay and the Land's End

Comprehending the Topography, Botany, Agriculture, Fisheries, Antiquities, Mining, Mineralogy and Geology of Western Cornwall

JOHN AYRTON PARIS

CAMBRIDGE
UNIVERSITY PRESS

CAMBRIDGE
UNIVERSITY PRESS

University Printing House, Cambridge, CB2 8BS, United Kingdom

Published in the United States of America by Cambridge University Press, New York

Cambridge University Press is part of the University of Cambridge.

It furthers the University's mission by disseminating knowledge in the pursuit of education, learning and research at the highest international levels of excellence.

www.cambridge.org
Information on this title: www.cambridge.org/9781108069960

© in this compilation Cambridge University Press 2014

This edition first published 1824
This digitally printed version 2014

ISBN 978-1-108-06996-0 Paperback

A GVIDE TO MOVNTS BAY AND LANDS END.

A

GUIDE

TO THE

MOUNT's BAY

AND THE

LAND's END;

COMPREHENDING THE

TOPOGRAPHY, BOTANY, AGRICULTURE, FISHERIES,
ANTIQUITIES, MINING, MINERALOGY
AND GEOLOGY OF

𝖂𝖊𝖘𝖙𝖊𝖗𝖓 𝕮𝖔𝖗𝖓𝖜𝖆𝖑𝖑.

SECOND EDITION.

To which is added, for the information of Invalids,

A DIALOGUE ON THE PECULIAR ADVANTAGES OF THE CLIMATES
OF PENZANCE, DEVONSHIRE, AND THE
SOUTHERN PARTS OF EUROPE.

By a PHYSICIAN.

" Auditque suis *tria* littora campis."

LONDON:

PRINTED AND PUBLISHED BY W. PHILLIPS,
GEORGE YARD, LOMBARD STR :
SOLD ALSO BY T. VIGURS, PENZANCE; AND W. AND C. TAIT,
EDINBURGH.

1824.

TO

THE VICE PATRONS, PRESIDENT,

VICE PRESIDENTS,

AND MEMBERS

OF

𝕿𝖍𝖊 𝕽𝖔𝖞𝖆𝖑 𝕲𝖊𝖔𝖑𝖔𝖌𝖎𝖈𝖆𝖑 𝕾𝖔𝖈𝖎𝖊𝖙𝖞 𝖔𝖋 𝕮𝖔𝖗𝖓𝖜𝖆𝖑𝖑,

THIS WORK IS INSCRIBED,

AS A HUMBLE, YET SINCERE TRIBUTE OF RESPECT,

FOR THE ZEAL AND LIBERALITY WITH WHICH THEY CONTINUE

TO UPHOLD

AN INSTITUTION

" WHICH HAS RENDERED THEIR HOME THE SCHOOL OF

SCIENCE,

AND THEIR NATIVE RICHES INCREASING SOURCES

OF PROSPERITY."

TO THE READER.

THIS little volume has been republished, at the earnest solicitation of numerous friends and applicants, and with such additions and improvements as the present extended state of information appeared to render necessary. In obeying this call, the author trusts that he may, in some degree, remove the prejudice to which the carelessness of his provincial compositor must, on the former occasion, have exposed the work.

Since the publication of the first Edition, PENZANCE, and the District of the Mount's Bay, have become objects of greatly increased interest; the successful establishment of the Geological Society,—the erection of commodious Sea Baths, —the growing confidence of the Public, and of

a

the medical profession, in the superior mildness of the climate,—and the general amelioration of every thing connected with the wants and comforts of a winter residence, have powerfully operated in augmenting the influx of strangers and invalids, into this formerly obscure, and comparatively neglected district. Such considerations, it will be acknowledged, were quite sufficient to sanction the propriety and expediency of the present undertaking, but the author must in candour allow, that they would scarcely have prevailed, had not another powerful motive been in silent but effectual co-operation—the "*Antiquæ vestigia Flammæ,*"—a secret lingering after the pursuits of Geology have, for once at least, seduced him from a resolution he had formed on quitting Cornwall,—that of abandoning a science which can never be pursued except with enthusiasm; but which, from its direction and tendency, is wholly incompatible with the duties of an anxious and laborious profession.

As the work is calculated for the guidance of those who may seek the shores of the Mount's Bay, for its genial atmosphere, the introduction

of some general observations upon the subject
of Climate, appeared essentially necessary. For
this purpose, the form of a Dialogue has been
preferred to that of a Didactic essay; by which
much circumlocution is avoided, while the only
interesting parts of the question are thus made
to appear in a more prominent and popular point
of view.

The Cornish Dialogue, introduced in the
Appendix, for the sake of illustrating the provincial Dialect, has been composed after the
model of the well known " *Tim Bobbin*," which
was written for the accomplishment of the same
object, with reference to Lancashire. From the
direction in which it came into the hands of the
author, he is inclined to consider it as an hitherto unpublished production of the celebrated Dr.
Walcott.———Valete.

CONTENTS.

INTRODUCTION.

OF THE MOUNT's BAY, AND THE LAND's END
DISTRICT.

(Page 1.)

x *Contents.*

EXCURSION I.

(*Page 45*)

TO SAINT MICHAEL's MOUNT.

EXCURSION II.

(*Page* 74)

TO THE LAND's END, LOGAN ROCK, &c.

EXCURSION III.

(*Page* 119)

TO BOTALLACK MINE ; CAPE CORNWALL ; AND THE
MINING DISTRICT OF SAINT JUST.

EXCURSION IV.

(*Page* 143)

TO SAINT IVES, HAYLE, HUEL ALFRED, &c.

EXCURSION V.

(*Page* 176.)

TO REDRUTH, AND THE MINING DISTRICTS IN ITS VICINITY.

Contents. xvii

EXCURSION VI.

(*Page* 214.)

TO KYNANCE COVE AND THE LIZARD POINT.

APPENDIX.

Part I.

APPENDIX.

Part II.

Drawn by F. Fenton

A GUIDE

MOUNT'S BAY

THE LAND's END.

INTRODUCTION.

Of the Mount's Bay, and the Land's End District.

At the most western extremity, and in the lowest latitude of Great Britain, is situated this delightful and justly celebrated Bay. It is bounded by an irregularly curved outline of many miles in extent, the extreme points of which constitute the well known promontory of the " *Lizard*," and the singular head-land, " *Tol-Pedn-Penwith*," near the " *Land's End*."

From the Lizard, the shores pass northward and westward, and gradually losing, as they proceed, their harsh and untamed features, swell

A

into sloping sweeps of richly cultivated land, and into hills glowing with the freshest verdure. As the coast advances, and at the same time spreads itself southward, it unites to its luxuriant richness a bolder character, and, rising like a vast amphitheatre, it opposes a barrier to western storms, while it presents its undulating bosom to the sun, and collecting his rays, pours them again with multiplied effect, upon every part of the surrounding country. The shores now pass westward, and extend to the *Land's End*, in their approach to which they become more rocky and precipitous, and occasionally exhibit some of the finest cliff scenery in the island, displaying by splendid natural sections the exact structure and relations of the rocks of which the country is composed.

The western shores are sprinkled with pictu-turesque villages, churches, cottages, and villas; and near the eastern margin of the bay, a pile of rocks, supporting a venerable chapel on its summit, starts abruptly from the waves, and presents an appearance of a most singular and beautiful description—this is *Saint Michael's Mount*, an eminence equally celebrated in the works of the poet, the naturalist, the antiquary, and the historian.

If we pursue the coast, and, turning round the western extremity of our island, trace its outline as it proceeds northerly, and then easterly to the *Bay of Saint Ives*, a very different country presents itself, instead of the undulating curves, and luxuriant herbage of the southern shores, the land is generally high,—the vallies short, narrow, and quick of descent, and the whole landscape affords a scene of incomparable cheerlessness; on the summit of almost every hill the granite is to be seen protruding its rugged forms in the most fantastic shapes, while the neighbouring ground is frequently covered for some distance with its disjointed and gigantic fragments, tumbled together in magnificent confusion; scarcely a shrub is seen to diversify the waste, and the traveller who undertakes to explore the more desolate parts of the district, will feel as if he were walking over the ruins of the globe, and were the only being who had survived the general wreck; and yet Ulysses was not more attached to his Ithaca, than is the Cornish peasant to his wild and cheerless dwelling.

" Dear is that shed to which his soul conforms,
" And dear that hill which lifts him to the storms."

Nor let the intelligent tourist despair of amusement, for he will find much to interest, much to

delight him.   There is not perhaps a district in
Great Britain which presents greater attractions
to the mineralogist or geologist; and there is
certainly not one which, in so small a compass,
has produced so many species of earthy and metallic minerals, or which displays so many geological varieties.   At the same time the antiquarian
may here occupy himself with the examination of
the rude relics of antiquity, which lie scattered
on all sides—nothing is more pleasing than that
sacred enthusiasm which is kindled in the mind
by the contemplation of the faded monuments of
past ages, and surely no spot was ever more congenial to such sensations.   But to return from
the digression.

THE CLIMATE of Mount's Bay is the circumstance which has principally contributed to its
celebrity, and is that which renders its shores so
beneficial to invalids.   Its seasons have been
aptly compared to the neap tides, which neither
ebb nor flow with energy; for, notwithstanding
its southern latitude, the summer is never sultry,
while the rigour of winter is so ameliorated that
thick ice * is rarely seen; frost, if it occurs, is but

---

* Skaiting, as an amusement, is entirely unknown among the
young men of Penzance.   The marsh between this place and
Marazion, which is generally overflowed in the winter season, and
which offers, when frozen, a very fair field for the skaiter, has not

of a few hours duration; and the snow storms which, coming from the north and east, bury the fields of every other part of England, are generally exhausted before they reach this favoured spot, or their last sprinkling is dissolved by the warm breezes which play around its shores.

The records lately collated and published by Dr. Forbes, from the meteorological journals of Messrs. Giddy, eminent surgeons at Penzance, afford abundant proof that this neighbourhood enjoys a mean summer temperature *under*, and a mean winter temperature greatly *above*, the mean of places similarly situated as to latitude, but differing in the latter being placed at a distance from the sea; for the mass of water held in the vast basin of the ocean preserves a far more even temperature than the atmosphere, and is constantly at work to maintain some degree of equilibrium in the warmth of the air; so that in the summer it carries off a portion of the caloric from it, while in the winter it restores a part of that which it contains. *

---

been more than four times during the last thirty years sufficiently solidified to admit of that diversion, viz. in the years 1788, 1794, 1814, and 1819.

* It is this fact that permits the cultivation of many species of plants in the open ground about London, which in the vicinity of Paris will not live without a green-house.

The same registers have, moreover, recorded a
fact with respect to the Penzance climate which
renders it still more acceptable to the invalid,—
the comparatively small annual, monthly, and
daily range of its temperature. Nor are the indications of the thermometer the only test upon
which we need rely,—the productions of nature
will furnish striking elucidations, and amply con-
firm the justness of our meteorological observations. From the vegetable kingdom we derive
conclusive evidence of the mildness of our winter, since all green-house plants may be preserved
with far less care and attendance than in any
other part of England; myrtles * and geraniums,
even of the tenderest kind, and many other exotics, are here constantly exposed during the winter, and yet they flower most luxuriantly in the
summer. The *Hydrangea* attains an immense
size in our shrubberies, as does also the *Verbena
Triphylla.* The great American aloe (*Agave
Americana*), has flowered in the open air at
Mousehole, at Tehidy park, and in the Scilly

---

* These plants thrive in the open air, and commonly attain a
height of ten or twelve feet; they may be seen trained on the front
of some of the houses in Penzance to double that height. A sufficient quantity of cuttings was obtained from a tree of this description, covering one of the houses, in the course of six weeks, to supply the oven with fuel for three months!

islands. To these we may add a long list * of
tender exotics, all of which are flourishing in the
neighbourhood of Penzance, and it has been justly
remarked that were ornamental horticulture to
become an object of attention in this neighbourhood, as it is in many other parts of England,
this list might be very considerably extended.
Amomgst the rare *indigenous* plants of this district, the *Sibthorpia Europœa* may be particu-
larised as affording a remarkable proof of the

---

* The following catalogue was drawn up by the *Rev. W. T. Bree,*
of Allesley, Warwickshire, *viz.*

Amaryllis Vittata.	Hydrangea Decolor.
Arum Colocasia.	Haustonia Coccinea.
Azalea Indica.	Hemerocallis Alba.
Buddlœa Globosa.	Lavandula Viridis.
Bocconia Cordata.	Lobelia Fulgens.
Coronilla Glauca, &c.	Myrtus Communis.
Calla Æthiopica.	Mesembryanthemum Deltoideum
Cistus Salvifolius.	Melianthus Major.
Chrysanthemum Indicum	Mimulus Glutinosus.
Camellia Japonica.	Magnolia Tripetala.
Cyclamen Persicum.	Metrosideros Lanceolata.
Canna Indica.	Olea Fragrans.
Cheiranthus Tristis.	Pittosporum Undulatum.
Dahlia (many varieties.)	Phylica Ericoides.
Daphne Indica.	Protœa Argentea.
Eucomis Striata.	Punica Nana.
Fuchsia Coccinea.	Solanum Pseudo-Capsicum.
Geranium (several species of	Teucrium Frutescens.
the African G.)	———— Marum.
Hypericum Coris.	Verbena Triphylla.
———— Crispum	Westringia Rosmarinacea.
———— Balearicum.	

mildness of our winter. This elegant little plant
when transplanted into the midland counties is
killed even in the most sheltered gardens. Nor
must we pass over unnoticed the more substantial
proofs of the same fact, as furnished by our winter markets, for at a season when pot-herbs of all
kinds are destroyed by frost in the eastern counties, our tables are regularly supplied in abundance ; * and so little is the progress of vegetation checked during the months of winter, that
the meadows retain their verdure, and afford even
a considerable supply of grass to the cattle.

Nor is the animal kingdom deficient in proofs
of the congenial mildness of western Cornwall.
We are indebted to the *Reverend W. T. Bree,* of

---

* *Cabbages* are ready for the table as early as February ; *Turnips*
before the end of March ; *Broccoli*, against Christmas ; *Green Peas*
are generally ready by the middle of May. But the most remarkable exception, perhaps, to the ordinary routine of the culinary
calendar is to be found in the growth of the potatoe. It is cus-
tomary for the gardeners in the vicinity of Penzance to raise two
crops in one year. The first being planted in November is gathered
in April, May, and June ; the second crop is planted immediately
on taking up the first, and as late as to the middle of July. The
first or spring crop has, in general, no other defence from the cold
of winter than the stable dung used as manure, and it is rarely
injured by the frost! Such is the ordinary practice of the market-
gardener ; but Mr. Bolitho of Chyandour, has constantly new pota-
toes at Christmas, and through the whole of January and part of
February, raised *in the open garden*, with no other shelter than that
afforded by some matting during the coldest nights.

Allesley, Warwickshire, for the following remarks, which were communicated by him to Dr.
Forbes of Penzance, and published by that gentleman in his Observations on the Climate of this
neighbourhood.

" One of the most remarkable instances of the
mildness of your climate is the unusually early
appearance of frog's spawn : this I observed at
Gulval on the 8th of January. According to
White's Naturalist's Calendar (which was made
from observations taken in Hampshire, a warm
and early county,) the earliest and latest appearances there specified, are February 28th, and
March 22d. Taking therefore the second week
in March as the average for its appearance, you
should seem, in this instance, to be full two
months earlier than Hampshire."

" In this neighbourhood (near Coventry) I
rarely see any of our species of Swallow, except
perhaps an occasional straggler, before the second
week in April, but in the year 1818 I was not a
little gratified at observing upwards of a score of
Sand Martins, (*Hirundo Riparia*), sporting over
the marsh between Gulval and Marazion, on
March 31st. The wind at that time was N. W.
and the thermometer at 50° in the shade at noon.
The Chaffinch (*Fringilla Cœlebs*) I heard, in

Cornwall, begin to chirp his spring note the last
day of December. With us he is seldom heard
until the beginning of February. The Viper,
(*Coluber Berus*), a great lover of warmth and
moisture, occurs more frequently in Cornwall
than in the midland counties."

We have already stated that our summers are
as remarkable for coolness, as our winters are desirable for mildness. This circumstance necessarily renders our fruit inferior in flavour to that
which is produced in the inland counties; indeed
the grape very rarely ripens in the open air, and
the apricot tree seldom affords any fruit, except
in a few favoured spots. The tree of the green-
gage plum is nearly equally unproductive. The
walnut, and the common hazel-nut very seldom
bear fruit. Apples for the table, however, are
plentiful and good; and our strawberries may be
considered as possessing a decided superiority.

Why then, it may be asked, should not this
climate be as eligible to invalids as that which
they are generally sent across the Channel to
enjoy? In reply we will venture to assert, and
without the least fear of being contradicted by
those, whose experience renders them competent
judges, that it is not only equally beneficial, but
far more eligible, unless, indeed, the patient can

possess himself of the cap of Fortunatus, to remove the difficulties and discomfiture of a continental journey. But since the present volume
is, in some measure, written for the information
and guidance of those who are seeking a winter's
residence, in pursuit of health, the author has
been induced to subjoin a short essay, in the appendix, for the purpose of examining the comparative pretentions of the several places to the
reputation for superior mildness and salubrity,
which they have acquired.

From the peninsular situation of Cornwall, and
its proximity to the Atlantic ocean, over which
the wind blows, at least, three-fourths of the
year, the weather is certainly very subject to
rain, and it is found that when other parts of
England suffer from drought, Cornwall has rarely
any reason to complain; this peculiarity seems
highly congenial to the inhabitants, as well as to
the soil; a Cornishman never enjoys better health
and spirits than in wet seasons, and there is a
popular adage, that " *the land will bear a shower
every day, and two upon a sunday*;" this, like most
of our popular sayings, although it requires to be
understood with some grains of allowance, is
founded on observation and experience. The
philosophical explanation of the fact is obvious;

the shallowness of the soil, and the large proportion of siliceous matter which enters into its composition, together with the nature of its rocky
substratum, necessarily render a constant supply
of moisture indispensable to its fertility. And
we here cannot but admire the intelligence displayed by Nature in connecting the wants and
necessities of the different parts of Creation with
the power and means of supplying them ; thus in
a primitive country, like Cornwall, where the
soil is constantly greedy of moisture, we perceive
that the rocks, elevated above the surface, solicit
a tribute from every passing cloud ; while in alluvial and flat districts, the soil of which is rich,
deep, and retentive of water, the clouds float
undisturbed over the plains, and the country very
commonly enjoys that long and uninterrupted
series of dry weather which is so congenial and
essential to its productions.

It deserves, however, to be noticed, that the
rains of Cornwall are, in general, rather frequent
than heavy.

> " Not such as wintry storms on mortals shed
> Oppressing life, but lovely, gentle, kind,
> And full of every hope, and every joy,
> The wish of Nature."——

It has been satisfactorily ascertained, by means
of the rain gauge, that the actual quantity of rain

that falls is rather under the mean of the whole
of England ; and Dr. Borlase observes that " we
have very seldom a day so thoroughly wet, but
that there is some intermission, nor so cloudy,
but that the sun will find a time to shine." This
circumstance may, perhaps, in part depend upon
the narrow, ridgelike form of the peninsula, over
which the winds make a quick, because they have
a short passage, and therefore do not suffer the
clouds to hang long in one place, as they frequently do in other situations; we are, besides,
much indebted to Ireland for this moderation of
the elements; she may be truly denominated the
Umbrella of Cornwall, for were not the vast body
of clouds, which the winds bring from the Atlantic, attracted and broken by her hills, we should
most probably be deluged with more constant and
excessive rain.

Notwithstanding the supposed moisture of the
Mount's Bay, the air is not less fit for respiration,
nor less beneficial to the valetudinarian, than that
of drier situations. The porous nature of the
shelfy substratum soon disposes of any excess of
water; so that, after a short cessation of rain,
the invalid may safely venture abroad to enjoy
the delightful walks which surround the bay; at
the same time, the numerous promontories which

distinguish this coast, promote a constant circulation of breezes around their extremities, so that mists seldom linger, and we never experience those sultry calms, or suffocating fogs, which not unfrequently infest other parts of our island.

As Cornwall is directly exposed to the expanse of the Atlantic ocean, lying south-west of it, we cannot be surprised that the winds, which blow so generally from that quarter, should occasionally produce very violent storms. Their approach is frequently predicted by the experienced fisherman, from the agitation of the water along shore, a phenomenon which is called a "*ground swell*;" and which is probably occasioned by a storm in the Atlantic, with the wind west; in which case, as the storm proceeds eastward, the waves raised by it will outgo the wind, and reach the eastern coast long before it. A tremendous instance of this kind occurred, during the residence of the author of these pages, on the night of Sunday, January 19th, 1817. The storm assumed the character of a hurricane, and acting in conjunction with a spring tide, impelled the waves with such fury, that they actually broke over the mast heads of the vessels which were lying within Penzance harbour, and bore down every thing before them; two of the four pillars recently erected

for the reception of a light were thrown down,
and several of the foundation stones of the pier
removed. The windows of the bath-house were
demolished, and the whole of its furniture washed
into the sea. The green between Penzance and
Newlyn was torn up, and several boats, lying on
the strand were actually carried into the neighbouring meadows. The towns of Newlyn and
Mousehole suffered corresponding damage, and
several of their houses were washed away. The
road between Marazion and St. Michael's Mount
was torn from its lowest foundation, and stones
of more than a ton in weight, though clamped
together with massy iron, were severed and removed from their situation. The turnpike road
between Penzance and Marazion was, in many
places, buried with sand; and in others, broken
up by the violence of the waves, and covered by
the sea to the depth of from three to five feet.
Had the violence of the storm lasted but a few
hours longer, who will venture to say that the
two channels would not have been united by the
inundation of the low land which constitutes the
isthmus, and the district of the Land's-end been
converted into an island!

The sea is encroaching upon every part of the
Cornish coast. In the memory of many persons

still living, the cricketers were unable to throw a ball across the " *Western Green*," between Penzance and Newlyn,* which is now not many feet in breadth, and the grandfather of the present vicar of Madron is known to have received tithes from the land under the cliff of Penzance. On the northern coast we have striking instances of the sea having made similar inroads. This however is the natural result of the slow and silent depredation of the water upon the land; but at a very remote period we are assured by tradition, that a considerable part of the present bay, especially that comprehended within a line drawn from near Cuddan point on the east side, to Mousehole on the west, was land covered with wood, but which, by an awful convulsion and irruption of the sea, was suddenly swept away. " If we trace the north-west shore of the bay, from the Mount westward to Newlyn, the ebb tide leaves a large space uncovered; the sea sand is from one to two or three feet deep; and under

---

* Mr. Boase has lately published, in the 2d volume of the Transactions of the Cornish Society, a very interesting letter upon this subject, (in the possession of Mrs. Ley of Penzance, who is the present representative of the Daniel family.) It was written, in the reign of Charles II, to the then proprietor of an estate, which included part of the " *Western Green*;" and that *part* is there estimated at *thirty-six acres of pasturage!*

this stratum of sand is found a black vegetable
mould, full of woodland detritus, such as the
branches, leaves, and nuts of coppice wood, together with the roots and trunks of forest trees
of large growth. All these are manifestly indigenous; and, from the freshness and preservation
of some of the remains, the inundation of sand,
as well as water, must have been sudden and
simultaneous; and the circumstance of ripe nuts
and leaves remaining together would seem to
shew that the irruption happened in the autumn,
or in the beginning of winter. This vegetable
substratum has been traced seaward as far as the
ebb would permit, and has been found continuous
and of like nature. Another proof of these shores
having been suddenly visited by a tremendous
catastrophe, has been afforded by the nature of
the sand banks constituting the " *Eastern,*" and
" *Western Greens,*" and which will be found to
be the detritus of disintegrated granite; whereas
the natural sand, which forms the bed of the sea,
is altogether unlike it, being much more comminuted, different in colour, and evidently the result
of pulverised clay-slate:" * but when did this
mighty catastrophe occur, and what were its

---

* See " A memoir on the submersion of part of the Mount's Bay,
by H. Boase, Esq." in the 2d volume of the Cornish Transactions.

causes? These are questions which are not readily answered; the event is so buried in the depths of antiquity, that nothing certain or satisfactory can be collected concerning it; although it would appear from the concurrent testimony of Florence of Worcester,* and the Saxon Chronicles, that a remarkable invasion of the ocean occurred in November 1099. With respect to the causes of the phenomenon we are equally uninformed; let the geologist examine the appearance of the coast with attention, and then decide with what probability De Luc attributed the catastrophe to a subsidence of the land. It must not, however be concealed that many geologists have questioned the probability of the occurrence altogether, and argue from the appearance of the coast, "whose rocks beat back the envious siege of watery Neptune," that no very important change in the hydrographical outline of the Cornish peninsula can have taken place, during the present constitution of the earth's surface. If Saint Michael's Mount be in reality the "*Ictis*"

---

* *On the third of the nones of November,*" cries Florence of Worcester, "*the sea comes out upon the shores, and buried towns and men, very many, oxen and sheep innumerable.*" While the Saxon Chronicle relates that "*this year eke, on Saint Martin's mass day, sprang up so much the sea flood, and so myckle harm did, as no man minded it ever afore did.*"

of Diodorus Siculus, we have certainly a decisive proof that no material change has taken place for the space of eighteen centuries at least; for the Historian describes the access to this island precisely such as it is at the present period—practicable only at low water for wheel carriages.

Nor is the corroding operation of the other elements upon the hills of Cornwall less evident and striking; no where are the vestiges of degradation more remarkable; granitic countries usually present a bold and varied outline, whereas the aspect of Cornwall, with some few exceptions, is comparatively tame, and even flat. "*I went into Cornwall,*" said a geologist of well known celebrity, "*to see an example of a primitive country; but, instead of an example, I found an exception.*" The same observation would apply to the agricultural character of the county, for its fertility is much greater than that which usually occurs in a country composed of primitive rocks.

All that peninsular portion of Cornwall which is situated to the westward of a line drawn from the estuary of Hayle on the north, to Cuddan point on the south, has been distinguished by the appellation of the *Land's End District.* It is about thirteen miles long from east to west,

and five or six miles broad from north to south,
and contains, by superficial admeasurement about
54,000 statute acres. It has been remarked that
the small extent of this district, and its peninsular
character, preclude the existence of rivers of any
magnitude; its varied and uneven surface, however, gives it a great profusion of small streams
and rivulets, which add greatly to its value. We
shall take occasion to introduce some remarks on
its agriculture, in our excursion to the Land's
End.

Penzance.

PENZANCE.

HAVING offered a rapid coup d'œil of the
country we are about to examine, we shall now
conduct the stranger into *Penzance*,* as being a

---

* Penzance signifies, in Cornish, *Holy-head*, i. e. *holy headland*;
and the town appears to have been so called in consequence of a
small chapel, dedicated to that universal patron of fishermen, Saint
Anthony, having formerly stood on the projecting point near the
present quay. When it became necessary to adopt arms for the
town, the true origin of its name was forgotten or overlooked, and
the holy head of Saint John emblazoned. It would, however, appear from the *Liber valorum*, that *Buriton* was the old name of

town well calculated to afford him an eligible residence; many of the various objects of interest are within the range of a morning's ride, and he will meet with every accommodation that may be required for the performance of his excursions; if his pursuit be mineralogy and geology, it is in this town that he will find others zealously engaged in the study of the same science, from whom he will readily obtain much local information; while in the collection of the Geological Society, so liberally opened for the inspection of every scientific stranger, he will see well defined specimens illustrative of the districts he may be desirous of exploring.

The reader of this Guide, therefore, must thoroughly understand that in the arrangement of the subsequent "Excursions," the various objects of interest, to which it directs him, are described in an order best adapted to the convenience of the resident at Penzance.

PENZANCE is the most western market town in the kingdom; about ten miles from the land's

---

Penzance,—a sound which to the ear of the antiquary is full of historical intelligence, for the addition of *Bury* to the name of a town signified that it was a town with a castle; thus, *Buriton* signified Bury-town, i. e. the Castle town. Some cellars near the quay are to this day called the *Barbican* cellars; thus tradition points out the castle to have been upon, or near, the site of the present chapel.

end, and 282 miles W. S. W. of London. It is beautifully situated on the north-west shore of the Mount's Bay, on a declivity jetting into the sea. The lands in its vicinity having a substratum of *hornblende rock* and *slate*, are not exceeded in fertility by any soil in the kingdom; a belt of land around the town, which consists of about a thousand acres, producing an annual rent of £10,000! The town is well defended by surrounding hills from the fury of Atlantic storms. It is large and populous, containing more than six thousand inhabitants. The Corporation* consists of a mayor, recorder, eight aldermen, and twelve common-council men; by whose funds, †　unaided by any parliamentary grant, a very commodious pier was erected about fifty years ago,

---

* Penzance was first incorporated in the reign of king James, in 1614; which charter was confirmed by Charles II.

† The history of these funds exhibits a curious instance of the increase in value which property undergoes, in a series of years, from the progressive improvements of the district in which it lies. The revenue of the Corporation, nearly £2000 per annum, is derived from an estate which was purchased from one Daniel, in the year 1614, for the sum of £34, and 20 shillings a year fee farm rent, payable out of the same to the vender and his representatives for ever. This estate is described in the writings to be "a three corner plot with a timber house (then) lately erected thereon, together with the tolls, profits, and dues of the fairs, markets, and of the pier." The increase of its value has arisen from the enlargement of the market now held on the spot, and from the dues arising from the improved and extended pier.

and which has lately been considerably extended,
so that it is now more than 600 feet in length, and
is the largest pier in Cornwall. It has, moreover, received the addition of a light which is
displayed every night, from half flood to half
ebb, and is consequently extinguished as soon as
there is less than nine feet of water within the
pier. At high water there is now at Spring tides
22 feet of water, * which is about five feet more
than that at the pier of Saint Michael's Mount.
The expenses incurred by these late improvements are to be paid by a new tariff, established
by an act passed in the year 1817.

The mother church is situated at Madron, but
there is a chapel of ease in the town, dedicated to
Saint Mary, the simple and unassuming spire of
which forms a very interesting object in the bay.

Besides the established church, there are several places of religious worship. The Wesleyan
Methodists' chapel, built in the year 1814, is the
most complete and capacious meeting-house in
the county. There are, morever, appropriate

---

* We are desirous of recording this fact since it continues to be
erroneously stated in the publication called the "*Coasting Pilot*,"
as well as in all charts, to be only 13 feet, as it was before the improvements. From the perpetuation of this error the masters of
vessels unacquainted with the place, refuse to credit the pilots,
when informed by them of the depth of the water.

places of worship for the Independents, Baptists, and Quakers, and a synagogue for the Jews.

Penzance is one of those towns to which the tinners bring their tin to be "*coined*" as it is called, that is, to be assayed and licensed by the officers of the Duchy, who take off a piece from the *corner* * of each block; and if they find it sufficiently pure, stamp the former with the Duke's arms. The stranger will be much struck by the singular sight of many thousand blocks of Tin, which lie in heaps, like worthless rubbish, about the street,† each weighing about 320 lb. and may perhaps be worth from £18 to £20. The Tin intended for the Mediterranean trade is here formed into bars, while that designed for exportation to the East Indies is cast into ingots.

There is a Public Dispensary, supported by the voluntary contributions of the inhabitants, aided occasionally by the donations of those invalid strangers, who, grateful for the reestablishment of health in themselves, eagerly adopt this mode of contributing to its restoration in others. Few

---

* The operation is termed "*Coining*," not, as is very generally supposed, from the stamping of the Duke's arms, but from the cutting off the *corner* of each block, from the French word *coin*, a *corner*. For every cwt. so stamped, the Duke receives four shillings, producing an annual revenue of £10,000.

† Since the first edition, the place of coinage has been changed from the middle of the town to a large area near the quay.

institutions for the accomplishment of a similar object, have proved more extensively beneficial; and none, we will venture to add, were ever superintended with more humane attention.

To the scientific visitor, Penzance possesses an interest of no ordinary degree. In the year 1814, DR. PARIS, who was at that time the resident physician, succeeded, through the support of the nobility, gentry, and mine agents of the county, in establishing a society for the cultivation and promotion of mineralogical and geological science; and, when we consider the immense advantages of its locality, the ability of its members, and the zeal and munificence of its patrons, we cannot be surprised to find that the short period of nine years has been sufficient to raise it to a respectable rank amongst the eminent institutions of this country. His present Majesty, having graciously condescended to become its patron, it is now denominated the ROYAL GEOLOGICAL SOCIETY OF CORNWALL. The Marquis of Hertford, Lord Warden of the Stannaries, and The Right Honourable Lord De Dunstanville, are its Vice-Patrons, and Davies Gilbert, Esq. M.P., the President; while amongst its officers and members it has enrolled the names of many individuals of the first rank and science in the kingdom. Two volumes of the Society's Transactions are already given to the public, from which a fairer estimate may be formed of the value of its labours, than from any sketch which the limited pages of this "*Guide*" could possibly afford; we shall, however, for the information of our scientific readers, present, in the *Appendix*, a list of the different memoirs which each volume contains. The splendid and extensive series of minerals, already exceeding four thousand specimens, which are deposited in an elegant and spacious museum,* offers a most honourable and durable testimony of the zeal and talent with which this department has been conducted; while to the student in mineralogy it affords a most desirable and solid system of instruction; indeed it has already excited such a spirit of inquiry among the miners, as to have led to the discovery of several minerals, before unknown in Cornwall.

There is also an œconomical department, con-

---

* The rooms originally occupied by the Society, and which are represented in the vignette at the head of this chapter, becoming too small to accommodate the growing collection, a capacious and handsome suite of rooms were erected in the year 1817; to which are now attached a public library, and a room for the reception of newspapers. The former was established in 1818, under the auspices of Sir Rose Price, Bart. and with the support of above a hundred subscribers in the neighbourhood.

taining specimens in illustration of the various changes which the ores of Tin, Copper, &c. undergo in the processes of dressing and smelting. Models are likewise to be seen of the machinery which is employed in such operations. The whole has been admirably arranged under the skilful direction of the Curator, *E. C. Giddy, Esq.*

In the geological department of the Museum are complete series of specimens illustrative of the serpentine formation of the *Lizard,*—of the slate formation of the " *Land's End District,*"— of the limestone formation of Veryan, and of the hornblende rocks of St. Cleer near Liskeard. There is besides an interesting series of " *Elvans*" * from different levels in many of the principal mines of the county, together with a collection of veins of metallic and earthy substances.

Among the earthy minerals, we may particularize, as unusually fine, the specimens of *Calcedony, Sodalite, Haüyne, Petalite, Colophonite, Vesuvian,* &c. In the metallic department, we may notice the *Carbonate of Lead, Specular Iron, Arseniate of Iron,* the *Oxide, Carbonate, Arseniate and Phosphate of Copper, Native Gold* from the Tin-stream-works of Cornwall, *Arsenical Pyrites,*

---

* See a paper " *On Elvan Courses,*" by J. Carne, Esq. in the first volume of the Royal Geological Society of Cornwall.

Uranite, Uran-ochre, Native Nickel, &c. Here also may be seen a mineral, hitherto almost un-known, *a Sub-carburet of Iron;* it was analysed by that late eminent chemist, the *Rev. W. Gregor,* who received it from the hands of the *Rev. J. Rogers* of Mawnan. It was found in a vein about half an inch wide, intersecting either hard *Clay-slate* or *Graywacké.* Among the saline mine-rals in the cabinet are *Glauberite,* and *Sassoline* or native Boracic acid.

A Laboratory, containing the necessary appa-ratus for analytical operations, is attached to the establishment.

In conclusion, we will venture to affirm, that the advantages and enjoyments which such socie-ties are calculated to afford are not only obtained without any expense to the country in which they are encouraged, but that they actually repay *in wealth* and *emolument* much more than they require for their support. Had the Cornish Society been earlier called into existence, we should never have heard of the most valuable productions of our country having been thrown into the sea, nor of their having been used as materials for the repair of roads, or the construc-tion of cottages: on the contrary, how many thousand tons of ore might have been gained?—

how many years of unprofitable but expensive labour saved? and how many individual adventurers preserved from disappointment, or rescued from ruin? Amongst the efforts made by this Society to improve the theory and art of mining, through the application of science, not the least interesting and praiseworthy is that which relates to the prevention of accidental explosion in the methods of blasting rocks with gunpowder, by the introduction of " *Safety Instruments.*"

How little aware is the great mass of the community at what an expense of human suffering and misery the ordinary necessaries of civilized life are obtained! Few of our readers, we will venture to say, have ever heard of the dreadful extent of the accidents which have occurred in the mines of Cornwall from the use of *iron* rammers, in the process of charging the rock with gunpowder, in order to blast it. Hundreds have been thus sent to an untimely grave, or, what perhaps is still worse, have been so mutilated as to remain blind and helpless objects of misery for the rest of their days, while their wives and children have been thus driven, in a state of destitution, to the hard necessity of seeking from charity that pittance which honest industry could no longer supply. We must refer the reader for

a full account of this appalling subject to Dr.
Paris's Memoir, in the first volume of the Society's
Transactions, entitled " *On the Accidents which*
occur in the Mines of Cornwall, in consequence of
the premature explosion of Gunpowder in blasting
rocks ; and on the methods to be adopted for pre-
venting it, by the introduction of a Safety Bar,
and an instrument termed the Shifting Cartridge."

We earnestly, therefore, entreat the Society to
persevere in those laudable efforts, which have
already ensured for it the respect of the learned,
and the gratitude of the public.—*Floreat.*

Besides the instructive collection of the Geological Society, the splendid cabinet of *Joseph Carne,*
Esq. may now be seen in this town, for since the
first edition of this " *Guide,*" the Cornish Copper
Company have given up their smelting establishment at Hayle, at which place *Mr. Carne* formerly lived as the resident partner. Among the
principal excellencies of this collection we may
notice *Prehnite,* in a variety of forms; *Axinite* in
the usual forms of that mineral; *Stilbite* in flat
four-sided prisms, terminated by pyramids; *Me-*
sotype radiated; *Garnets* in twelve, and twenty-
four sided crystals; *Pinite* in six and twelve sided
prisms; *Uranite* in quadrangular tables with the
angles sometimes truncated, and also in forms

much resembling cubes and octohedrons; *Uran-*
ochre; Native Bismuth; and *Specular Iron ore,*
little inferior in beauty to that brought from
Elba,—all of which are from Saint Just. From
other parts of Cornwall are *Sulphate of Lead*
(Vellenoweth Mine) in a variety of forms, more
especially in one resembling an octahedron;
Grey Sulphuret of Copper (Crenver mine), the
best defined crystals of which are very obtuse
dodecahedrons, and six sided prisms; in some
specimens the dodecahedron is so placed upon
the summit of a prism as to produce the whimsical appearance of a nail, which from its rarity
is sought after by mineral collectors with considerable avidity. Two specimens of rarity also
in this collection are the *Yellow*, and *Grey Sul-*
phuret of Copper, in forms approaching that of
Cube; the latter is pseudomorphous.

The Penwith Agricultural Society holds its
meetings, and distributes its premiums, in this
town. Nothing can be more in place than such
an institution. Geology and Agriculture are
kindred sciences, and it has been truly observed
that there is no district in the British Empire
where the natural relations between the varieties
of soil and the subjacent rocks can be more easily
discovered and traced, or more effectually inves-

tigated, than in the county of Cornwall; and no where can the information which such an enquiry is capable of affording, be more immediately and successfully applied for the improvement of waste lands, and the general advancement of agricultural science.

The market of Penzance, for the goodness, variety, and cheapness of its commodities, is certainly not surpassed by any other in the kingdom; to the great quantity of salt usually mixed with the food of the swine, is perhaps to be attributed the delicacy and richness of the pork; whilst, owing to the fine pasturage of the neighbourhood, the heifer beef is superior, beyond comparison, to the Scotch. It is worthy also of notice, that during the winter season the market is filled with a variety of wild-fowl, woodcocks, snipes, &c. which are offered for sale at extremely low prices. The market is held on Thursdays and Saturdays; but every description of fish in season, as *Red Mullet, John Doree, Turbet, Sole, Mackarel, Whiting, Pilchard, Herring,* &c. &c. may be purchased from the Newlyn fish-women, who are in daily attendance at their stalls, and whose fine symmetry, delicate complexions, curling ringlets, and the brilliancy of whose jet black eyes, as they dart their rays from beneath the

c

shade of large gypsey hats of beaver, fill the traveller with admiration.

We beg leave to introduce the reader to two
of these *Nymphs of Cowel.**

Whilst speaking of the delicacies of the table
we must not omit to mention the *clotted* or *clouted*
cream of this and the neighbouring county, †
a luxury with which the epicures of other parts
are wholly unacquainted.

The town of Penzance is rapidly extending
itself; new houses are continually rising in commanding situations; and, since the publication of
the first edition of this work, HOT AND COLD
SEA BATHS have been completed upon a suitable

---

* The *Cowel* is the provincial name of the peculiar basket in
which they convey their fish, and is carried by means of a string
round their hats, as represented above. Its name has been supposed to have been derived from its resemblance in position and
appearance to the Monk's *cowl.*

† The custom of obtaining the cream from new milk by coagu-
lation from heat, is peculiar to Devonshire, Cornwall, and the opposite coast of Brittany, and is supposed to be of Celtic origin.
The butter obtained by beating up this cream does not differ much
in flavour from that procured by churning new cream, except the
process be carelessly conducted, when it will acquire a smoky taste.

scale of convenience. The waiting room belonging to this establishment commands a prospect
of very singular beauty. St. Michael's Mount
rising boldly in front, forms a striking relief to
the extended line of coast which constitutes the
back ground; while the undulating shores on
the left, skirted by the little village of Chy'andour, are well contrasted, on the opposite side,
with the busy scene of the pier, and the numerous vessels in the harbour.

In enumerating the advantages this town holds
out as a residence to invalids, it deserves notice
that a packet sails every Friday to the Scilly
Islands, and returns on the following Tuesday.
The distance is about fourteen leagues, and, with
a fair wind, the passage is generally accomplished
in six hours; but with contrary winds it has
sometimes, though very rarely, exceeded two days.

In a town so remote from the metropolis, and
in a great degree insulated from the other parts
of the empire, it is not extraordinary that we
should find the traces of several very ancient
customs. The most singular one is, perhaps, the
celebration of the Eve of Saint John the Baptist,*

---

* It is reasonable to advert to the Summer Solstice for this custom, although brought into the Christian Calendar under the
sanction of John the Baptist. Those sacred fires "kindled about
midnight, on the moment of the Solstice by the great part of the

our town saint, which falls on Midsummer Eve;
and that of the Eve of Saint Peter, the patron of
fishermen. No sooner does the tardy sun sink
into the western ocean than the young and old of
both sexes, animated by the genius of the night,
assemble in the town, and different villages of
the bay, with lighted torches. Tar barrels having been erected on tall poles in the market
place, on the pier, and in other conspicuous spots,
are soon urged into a state of vivid combustion,
shedding an appalling glare on every surrounding
object, and which when multiplied by numerous
reflections in the waves, produce at a distant
view a spectacle so singular and novel as to defy
the powers of description; while the stranger
who issues forth to gain a closer view of the festivities of the town, may well imagine himself
suddenly transported to the regions of the furies
and infernal gods; or, else that he is witnessing,
in the magic mirror of Cornelius Agrippa, the
awful celebration of the fifth day of the Eleusinian Feast; * while the shrieks of the female

---

ancient and modern nations. The origin of which loses itself in
antiquity;" See *Gebelin*, and also *Brand's Observations on Popular
Antiquities*.

 * The fifth day of the Eleusinian feast was called " *the day of
the Torches*," because at night the men and women ran about with
them in imitation of Ceres, who having lighted a torch at the fire

spectators, and the triumphant yells of the torch bearers, with their hair streaming in the wind, and their flambeaus whirling with inconceivable velocity, are realities not calculated to dispel the illusion. No sooner are the torches burnt out than the numerous inhabitants engaged in the frolic, pouring forth from the quay and its neighbourhood, form a long string, and, hand in hand, run furiously through every street, vociferating " an eye,"—" an eye,"—" an eye" ! At length they suddenly stop, and the two last of the string, elevating their clasped hands, form *an eye* to this enormous *needle,* through which the *thread* of populace runs; and thus they continue to repeat the game, until weariness dissolves the union, which rarely happens before midnight.

On the following day *(Midsummer day)* festivities of a very different character enliven the bay; and the spectator can hardly be induced to believe that the same actors are engaged in both dramas. At about four or five o'clock in the afternoon, the country people, drest in their best apparel, pour into Penzance from the neighbour-

---

of Mount Ætna, wandered about from place to place, in search of her daughter Proserpine. Hence may we not trace the high antiquity of this species of popular rejoicing.

ing villages, for the purpose of performing an aquatic divertisement. At this hour the quay and pier are crowded with holiday-makers, where a number of vessels, many of which are provided with music for the occasion, lie in readiness to receive them. In a short time the embarkation is completed, and the sea continues for many hours to present a moving picture of the most animating description.

Penzance is remarkable in history for having been entered and burnt by the Spaniards, in the year 1595. From time immemorial a prediction had prevailed, that a period would arrive when " *Some strangers should land on the rocks of Merlin, who should burn Paul's Church, Penzance, and Newlyn.*" Of the actual accomplishment of this prediction we receive a full account from Carew, from which it would appear that on the 23d of July, 1595, about two hundred men landed from a squadron of Spanish gallies, on the coast of Mousehole, when they set fire to the church of Paul, and then to Mousehole itself. Finding litte or no resistance, they proceeded to Newlyn,* and from thence to Penzance. Sir Francis Godolphin endeavoured to inspire the

---

* Will not this historical fact explain the peculiar cast of beauty possessed by many of the Fish-women residing in this village.

inhabitants with courage to repel these assail-
ants; but, so fascinated were they by the remem-
brance of the ancient prophecy, that they fled in
all directions, supposing that it was useless to
contend against the destiny that had been predicted. The Spaniards availing themselves of
this desertion, set it on fire in different places,
as they had already done to Newlyn, and then
returned to their galleys, intending to renew the
flames on the ensuing day; but the Cornish having recovered from their panic, and assembled in
great numbers on the beach, so annoyed the
Spaniards with their bullets and arrows, that
they drew their galleys farther off, and availing
themselves of a favourable breeze, put to sea
and escaped.

It is worthy of remark, that when the Spaniards
first came on shore, they actually landed on a
rock called " *Merlin.*" The historian concludes
this narrative by observing that these were the
only Spaniards that ever landed in England as
enemies.

In recalling the historical events which have
invested this town with interest, we had nearly
omitted to state, that a tradition exists here, that
Tobacco was first smoked by *Sir Walter Raleigh*
in Penzance, on his landing from America. By

the Philosopher of a future age Penzance will,
doubtless, as the birth place of the illustrious
Sir Humphry Davy, be regarded with no
ordinary share of interest; and to those who may
be led to perform a pilgrimage to the early laboratory of this highly gifted philosopher, the vignette at the head of the present chapter will be
found materially useful in directing his steps. *

It would be inconsistent with the plan and
objects of the present work to enter into the details of biography, that duty must be reserved for
an abler pen, we shall therefore only state that
the present distinguished President of the Royal
Society was born in this town in the year 1779,
and that after having received the earlier part of
his education under *Dr. Cardew* at Truro, he was
placed with a respectable professional gentleman
of Penzance, of the name of *Tonkin*, in order
that he might acquire a knowledge of the profession of a surgeon and apothecary. His early
proofs of genius, however, having attracted a
gentleman well known for his strong perception
of character, he was fortunately removed to a
field better calculated to call forth the latent

---

* The house is the first on the left of the ascending footway, and
its only two small windows visible in the vignette, are situated immediately beneath the clock of the market house tower.

energies of his mind. The result is too well
known to require comment.

In the vicinity of the town are delightful walks
through shady dingles, and over swelling hills,
from whose summits we catch the most delicious
sea and land prospects; and which are not a
little heightened in beauty and effect by the glowing aerial tints so remarkably displayed in this
climate at the rising and setting of the sun. Here
too the Botanist may cull, in his rambles, a great
variety of rare indigenous plants; with a catalogue* of which we shall now close the present
chapter.

—◆◆—

LIST OF INDIGENOUS PLANTS OF
WESTERN CORNWALL.

Alisma Damasonium (*Star-headed Water Plantain*) between Pen-
zance and Marazion.
A——— Ranuncoloides. Marazion Marsh.
Anchusa Officinalis (*Common Alkanet*) St. Ives, &c.
Anethum Fœniculum, common near Marazion.
A——— Graveolens. Marazion Marsh.
Aquilegia Vulgaris (*Common Columbine*) St. Ives, Goldsithney, &c.
Antirrhinum Orontium (*Lesser Snapdragon*) Gulval, Land's End.
A——— Montspessilanum (*Bee Orchis*) Penhryn.
Anthemis Nobilis (*Common Chamomile*) *passim.*

---

* Many of these plants were enumerated in the former edition of
this work, to which are now added some others, from the catalogue
published by Dr. Forbes, in his observations on the climate of
Penzance.

Anthyllis Vulneraria (*dwarf with a red flower.*) (*Kidney-Vetch.*
Ladies' Finger.*) Downs, Whitsand Bay.

Aspidium Oriopteris (*Heath Shield-fern*) Gear Slamps and New
Mill.

Aspidium Dilatatum. Variety. (*Great Crested ditto*) Moist Banks.

Asplenium Marinum (*Sea Spleenwort*) St. Michael's Mount, Land's
End, Logan rock.

A———— Lanceolatum (*Lanceolate ditto*) Gulval, St. Michael's
Mount, Lemorna Cove, &c.

Bartsia Viscosa (*Yellow Viscid Bartsia*) Corn-fields near Hayle.

Brassica Oleracea (*Sea Cabbage*) Cliffs, Penzance.

Briza Minor (*Small Quaking-grass*) Cornfields between Gulval and
Ludgvan.

Bunias Cakile (*Sea Rocket*) Beach between Penzance and Newlyn.

Campanula Hederacea (*Ivy-leaved Bell-flower*) Trevaylor Bottom,
Gear Stamps, &c.

Chironia Littoralis (*Sea Centaury*) Beach between Penzance and
Marazion.

Cochlearia Officinalis (*Common Scurvy-grass*) Cliffs near the Sea,
common.

Convolvulus Soldanella (*Sea Bindweed*) Whitsand Bay, Marazion
Green.

Cucsuta Epithymum (*Lesser Dodder*) common upon Gorse.

Cynosurus Echinatus (*Rough Dog's-tail Grass*) Ludgvan.

Daucus Maritimus (*Wild Carrot*) Land's End, Logan rock, Botallack, &c.

Dicranum Cerviculatum (*Red-necked Forked Moss*) Gulval. Scilly.

D———— Crispum (*Curled ditto*) St. Mary's, Scilly.

Drosera Longifolia (*Long-leaved Sun-dew*) Marsh between Marazion and Penzance.

Erica Vrgans (*Cornish Heath*) Lizard Peninsula.

Erodium Maritimum (*Sea Stork's Bill*) Sea shore, common.

E———— Cicutarium (*Hemlock's Stork's Bill*) ditto.

Eryngium Maritimum (*Sea Holly*) Sea shore, common.

Euphorbia Peplis (*Purple Spurge*) Marazion Green.

———————— Portlandica (*Portland ditto*) Scilly Islands.

Exacum Filiforme (*Least Gentianella*) Marazion Marsh, beyond the
half way houses.

Genista Pilosa (*Hairy Green-weed*) Kynance Cove.

Gentiana Campestris (*Field Gentian*) Downs, Whitsand Bay.
Lizard, &c.

Geranium Columbinum (*Long-stalked Cran's-bill*) Ludgvan.

G———— Sanguineum (*Bloody Crane's-bill*) Kynance Cove.

Glaucium Luteum (*Yellow Horned Poppy*) Scilly Islands.

Helleborus Viridis (*Green Hellebore*) between Rosmorran and Kenegie, near the brook.

Herniaria Hirsuta (*Hairy Rupture-wort*) between Mullion and the Lizard.

Hookeria Lucens (*Shining Feather-moss*) Trevaylor Bottom. Between Rosmorran and Kenegie.

Hymenophyllum Tunbridgense (*Filmy-leaved fern*) Among the loose stones at Castle An Dinas, on the east side.

Hypnum Scorpioides (*Scorpion Feather-moss*) Gulval, Zennor, &c.

H———— Alopecurum, variety (*Fox-tail ditto*) Gulval.

Illecebrum Verticillatum (*Whorled Knott-grass*) Gulval. Gear Stamps, Land's end.

Inula Helenium (*Elecampane*) Gulval, The Mount, St. Ives, Scilly.

Iris Fœtidissima (*Stinking Iris, Roast Beef Plant*) Madron.

Linum Angustifolium (*Narrow-leaved pale Flax*) St. Ives.

L———— Usitatissimum. Near Redruth.

Littorella Lacustris (*Plantain Shoreweed.*) In a watery lane near Penzance.

Mentha Odorata (*Bergamot Mint*) Burian.

M———— Rotundifolia (*Round-leaved Mint.*) Between P nzance and Newlyn, Whitsand Bay.

Myrica Gale (*Sweet Gale. Dutch Myrtle*) Marsh, Gulval, and Ludgvan.

Neckera Heteromalla (*Lateral Neckera*) Trevaylor Bottom, Try, &c.

Neottia Spiralis. Between Penzance and Marazion.

Orchis Pyramidalis (*Pyramidal Orchis*) near Hayle.

Ornithogalum Umbellatum (*Common Star of Bethlehem*) near Marazion.

Ornithopus Perpusillus (*Common Bird's-foot*) Gulval, Carne, &c.

Osmunda Regalis (*Royal Moonwort*) Poltair.

Panicum Dactylum (*Creeping Panick Grass*) Marazion Beach.

Pinguicula Lusitanica (*Pale Butterwort*) Bogs in the neighbourhood.

Pyrethrum Maritimum (*Sea Feverfew*) Sea-shore.

Rubia Peregrina (*Wild Madder*) Hayle-Helston, &c.

Reseda Luteola (*Wild Woad, Dyer's Weed*) Coarse lands beyond
  Marazion.
Rumex Sanguineus (*Bloody-veined Dock*) Gulval.
Ruscus Aculeatus (*Butcher's Broom*) Lemorna Cove, &c.
Salvia Verbenacea (*Wild English Clary*) St. Ives, Scilly, &c.
Samolus Valerandi (*Brook-weed* or *Water Pimpernel*) Land's end,
  &c.
Santolina Maritima (*Sea Cotton weed*) Marazion beach.
Saponaria Officinalis (*Soap-wort*) St. Levan, Tresco Island, Scilly.
Saxifraga Stellaris (*Hairy Saxifrage*) Logan rock.
Scilla Verna (*Vernal Squill*) St. Ives, near Zennor, Morvah, oppo-
  site to Three Stone Oar.
Scirpus Fluitans (*Floating Club Rush*) Gulval Marsh.
Scutellaria Minor (*Lesser Skull-cap*) Bogs, Gulval.
Scrophularia Scorodonia (*Balm-leaved Figwort*) St. Ives, Gulval,
  and Chyandour, plentifully.
Sedum Anglicum (*English Stonecrop*) very common.
———— Telephium (*Orpine* or *Livelong*) Logan rock.
Sibthorpia Europœa (*Cornish Moneywort*) Moist banks, Gulval,
  Madron Well, Trereife Avenue ; Helston, &c.
Silene Anglica (*English Catchfly*) common in Cornfields.
Solidago Virgaurea (*Common Golden-rod*) Penzance, &c.
Spergula Nodosa (*Knotted Spurrey*) near Marazion.
Spiræa Filipendula (*Common Dropwort*) Kynance Cove.
Stachys Arvensis (*Corn Woundwort*) Cornfields, common.
Tamarix Gallica (*French Tamarisk*) The Mount-Lizard, Scilly
  Islands, but very probably introduced.
Trichostomum Polyphyllum (*Fringe Moss*) Gulval, Kenegie, &c.
Trifolium Subterraneum (*Subterraneous Trefoil*) near the Sea-shore.
Verbascum Nigrum (*Dark Mullein*) Gulval.
Utricularia Vulgaris (*Common Bladderwort*) between Rosmorran
  and Kenegie.

EXCURSION I.

TO SAINT MICHAEL's MOUNT.

=====

" This precious stone, set in the silver sea ! "

Richard II. Act 2. *scene* 1.

=====

THE traveller no sooner catches a glimpse of this extraordinary feature in the bay, than he becomes impatient to explore it; anticipating this feeling we have selected it as an object for his first excursion, and in its performance we promise him an intellectual repast of no ordinary kind.

To proceed to the Mount, by sea, the stranger may embark at Penzance pier, from which it is not more than two miles distant; by this arrangement an opportunity will be afforded for witnessing a fine panoramic view of the coast; should, however, his inclination, or the " tyranny of the winds and waves" oppose this project, he may proceed by land through the little village of

Chy'andour, over a semicircular beach covered with fine sand of about three miles in extent. Between this sand and the high road is the " *Eastern Green*," celebrated as the habitat of some rare plants, viz. *Panicum Dactylum* (in a line with Gulval church); *Chironia Littoralis; Alisma Damasonium; Neottia Spiralis; Euphorbia Peplis; Euphorbia Paralias; SantolinaMaritima; Convolvulus Soldanella,* &c. On the beach the Conchologist may collect some fine specimens of the *Echinus Cordatus,* which is the only shell ever found there. In the marshes on the left side of the road the common observer will be struck with the extreme luxuriance of the *Nymphæa alba,* while the Botanist may reap an ample harvest of interesting plants, viz. splendid specimens of *Montia Fontana,* as large as the figure of Micheli; *Illecebrum Verticillatum; Sison Inundatum; Apium Graveolens;* a rare variety of *Senechio Jacobæa; Alisma Ranunculoides; Stellaria Uliginosa; Pinguicula Lusitanica; Scirpus Fluitans; Exacum Filiforme; Drosera Longifolia; Scutellaria Minor; Myrica Gale,* &c.

Before our arrival at Saint Michael's Mount, the only intermediate object worthy of notice is the town of MARAZION, or MARKET JEW as it is sometimes called. It stands upon the sea shore, on the eastern shoulder of the bay, and is well sheltered from cold winds by a considerable elevation of land to the north; still, however, as it is exposed to the south-west, which is the prevailing wind, it is far less eligible as a place of residence for invalids than Penzance.

The town contains more than 1100 inhabitants; its principal support, if not its origin, according to some authors, was derived from the resort of pilgrims and other religious devotees to the neighbouring sacred edifice on Saint Michael's Mount; but its name was indisputably derived from the Jews who traded here several centuries ago, and held an annual *market* for selling various commodities, and purchasing tin, and other merchandize in return. In the reign of Queen Elizabeth it obtained a charter, vesting its government in a mayor, eight aldermen, and twelve capital burgesses, with a power to hold a weekly market, and two annual fairs. In the preamble to this charter it is stated " that Marghaisewe was a trading borough town of great antiquity, and that it suffered considerable dilapidation in the days of Edward VI., when a number of rebellious people entered, and took possession of the town, and laid many of the buildings in ruin." From this disaster the town does not appear to have ever recovered, while from the growing importance of Penzance, the suppression of the Priory, and the loss of the Pilgrims, from whom it derived its principal resources, its consequence gradually declined, until at length it dwindled into its present condition.

It has been asserted on good authority, that under this charter of Elizabeth, the town formerly sent members to Parliament, and *Dr. Borlase* in his manuscripts, mentions the names of *Thomas Westlake*, and *Richard Mills, Esqrs.* as those of the two members who were actually returned for Marazion in the year 1658. It does not, however, appear that they ever took their seats. It would seem, moreover, from some original letters which passed between the Sheriff of Cornwall and the mayor of this borough, during the protectorate of Cromwell, that the inhabitants were solicitous to recover their long neglected rights; but this effort proved ineffectual.

In going from Marazion to the Mount, we pass a large insulated rock, known by the name of the " *Chapel Rock*," whereon the Pilgrims, who came to visit the Priory of Saint Michael, are said to have performed certain devotionary and superstitious ceremonies, in a kind of initiatory chapel, previous to their admission to the more sacred Mount; there is not, however, the slightest vestige of any masonry to be discovered, and it would therefore seem more probable that it merely derived its name from its vicinity to the shrine of Saint Michael. The rock is composed of well marked *Greenstone*, resting on a bed of *clay slate*, and which, in its direction and dip, will be found to correspond with the slaty rock on the western base of the Mount.

We arrive at Saint Michael's Mount. — The rock of which it is composed is of a conical form; gradually diminishing from a broad, craggy base, towards its summit, which is beautifully terminated by the tower of a chapel, so as to form a pyramidal figure. On its eastern base, is a small fishing town, holding about 250 inhabitants; and a commodious pier,* capable of containing fifty sail of small vessels, and which proves to the proprietor of the Mount a considerable source of revenue.

The height from low water mark to the top of the chapel tower is about 250 feet, being 48 feet higher than the monument in London. In cir-

---

* This Pier has lately been considerably enlarged at the expense of Sir John St. Aubyn. The work was completed only in the last Summer (1823), and will now admit vessels of five hundred tons burthen.

cumference at the base, the Mount measures
nearly a mile, and is said to contain about seven
acres of land; such, however, is the effect of the
vast extent of horizon, and the expanded tract
of water which rolls around its base, that its
real magnitude is apparently lost.

In a mineralogical point of view, this eminence
is certainly the most interesting in Cornwall, or
perhaps in England; who can believe that this
little spot has occasioned greater controversy,
and more *ink*-shed than any mountain in the
globe? yet such is the fact; let us therefore before we ascend walk around its base and examine
the geological structure which has excited so
much attention. The scenery too is here of the
most magnificent description; rocks overhang
rocks in ruinous grandeur, and appear so fear-
fully equipoised, that, although secure in their
immensity, they create in the mind the most
awful apprehension of their instability, whilst
the mighty roar of the ocean beneath, unites in
effect with the scenery above.—All around is
sublime. —— But the Geology, enough of the
picturesque.

The body of the rock is composed of *Slate* and
Granite; the whole northern base consists of the
former, but no where does it extend to any

height, the upper part, in every direction, consisting of *Granite*. On the south side this *Granite*
descends to the water's edge, and it continues to
constitute the whole of the hill, both on the eastern and western side, for about three-fourths of
its whole extent. Where the granite terminates
numerous veins of it appear in the slate, in many
different directions; while the granite in its turn,
encloses patches of slate. In the vicinity of the
former rock the latter is found to contain so
much *Mica*, as to resemble *Micaceous Schist*, or
fine grained *Gneiss*, for which it has been erroneously taken by some of our earlier observers.
And, while at some of these junctions there would
seem to be a mere apposition of the two rocks,
at others, the intermixture is so complete as to
render it difficult to say to which of the two certain considerable masses belong.

Here then is the phenomenon which has invested the spot with so much geological interest.
Here is *Granite*, which *Werner* conceived to be a
primary formation, and around which he supposed all other rocks to have been deposited, if
not of a later date, at least contemporaneous, in
origin, with slate. How is this anomaly to be
explained? *De Luc* at once asserts what we
presume no rational observer can for one moment

believe, that the rock of which these veins are composed is *not* true Granite, but " *Pseudo-granite*" *!* *Dr. Berger* attempts to surmount the difficulty by a different expedient, and declares that *they are not veins !* but prominences from the granite beneath, which have been filled up by the subsequent deposition of clay-slate. It might, says *Sir H. Davy*,* with nearly as much reason be stated, that the veins of copper and tin belong to a greater interior metallic mass, and that they existed prior to the rocks in which they are found. The advocates of the Plutonian theory have, as might have been supposed, eagerly availed themselves of the support which this phenomenon is so well calculated to afford their favourite doctrine. They accordingly affirm that the granite has been raised up through the incumbent slate, into whose fissures it has insinuated itself. Upon these theories we shall offer no comment; it is the humble task of a " Guide" merely to direct the attention of the traveller to the phenomena themselves, and then to leave him to deduce his own conclusions from their appearance. In the fulfilment of this duty we recommend the geologist to proceed to the western base of the Mount, where he will find near

---

* Transactions of the Royal Geological Society of Cornwall, Vol. i. p. 41

the waters' edge, what have been considered by
Dr. Thomson as " two large beds of granite in
the slate, with veins running off from them; the
position and appearance of which are such as to
leave no doubt but that the great body of the
granite has been deposited posterior to the slate
formation." *Mr. Carne,* on the other hand, con-
tends that " these granite bodies cannot with
any propriety be called ' *Beds in the Slate*'; " one
of them," says he, " is a granitic vein, and although six feet wide near the granite mass, it
becomes gradually smaller as it recedes, and
dwindles to a point at the distance of 80 feet.
The other is a part of the granitic mass, from
which some veins appear to diverge; and, in *no
part* does it overlie the slate." *

The whole body of the Granite of the Mount
is traversed by an uninterrupted series of quartz
veins, which run parallel to each other with
wonderful regularity. They are very nearly vertical, and their direction is east and west. On
the north-east side of the Mount many of them
can be traced into the incumbent slate; a circumstance which strongly supports the idea of
the cotemporaneous origin of these two rocks.
In the investigation of these veins the Mineralo-

* Transactions of the Royal Geological Society of Cornwall,
Vol. ii. p. 73.

gist may pass many an hour with satisfaction, we shall therefore point out some of the more leading phenomena which deserve his attention. *De Luc* observed that " that part of the vein termed in Cornwall the *Capel,* and on the Continent *Selebanque,* and which is the first stratum adherent to the sides of the fissures, changes as it passes through different kinds of strata, sometimes consisting of white *Quartz,* sometimes of *Mica.*" *Dr. Forbes* * says, that occasionally, though rarely, the line of division between the vein and the rock is tolerably distinct; frequently, however, there is rather an insensible gradation of the matter of the one into that of the other, than an obvious apposition of surfaces." The exterior parts of the veins consist of a bluish *quartz,* very compact, and uniformly containing a great deal of *Schorl.* This *schorlaceous* character is much more distinct towards the sides or walls of the veins, their centre being generally pure *quartz ;* and, commonly, crystallized. In most of the veins there is a central line, or fissure, which divides them into two portions; this is formed by the close apposition and occasional union of

---

* Transactions of the Royal Geological Society of Cornwall, Vol. ii. p. 369.

two crystallized, or, as they may be called, *drusy* surfaces.

Since Veins must be considered as having once been the most active laboratories of Nature, so may they now be regarded as her most valuable cabinets of mineralogy. In those of Saint Michael's Mount may be found crystals of *Apatite*, from a very light to a very dark green colour, and exhibiting most of the modifications of form* which are common to that mineral; *Oxide of Tin; Felspar; Mica* beautifully crystallized in tables; *Topaz* in small whitish or greenish crystals,† both translucent and opaque, and which are extremely numerous, many hundred being observable on the face of some small blocks of granite that have fallen from the precipices.

Pinite has been said to have been also discovered in this spot. Besides which may be found that rare mineral, *the Triple Sulphuret of Cop-*

---

* See MR. PHILLIPS's "ELEMENTARY INTRODUCTION TO MINE-RALOGY." We shall on all occasions refer to this work without reserve, as being a book which is, or ought to be, in the hands of every scientific traveller. Its copious catalogue of English *habitats* renders it extremely valuable.

† The mineralogist is apt to overlook these Topazes, or to regard them as common *quartz crystals*, to which they bear a great resemblance, until we inspect their prisms, which will rarely be found to be six-sided; there is also another simple mark of distinction—in the *quartz* crystal the striated appearance on its surface is horizontal, whereas on the *Topaz* it is longitudinal.

per, *Antimony*, and *Lead; Sulphuret of Tin;*
Malachite; Fluor Spar; and *Wolfram.* The
occurrence of this latter mineral was, we believe,
first noticed in the earlier edition of the present
work, and is important in as far as its presence
is generally supposed to afford decisive evidence
of the primitive formation of the mountain masses
in which it occurs.

This spot also presents us with several lodes
of *Tin* and *Copper*; the latter may be traced for
a considerable distance from the eastern to the
southern base of the hill. The *lode* of Tin was
formerly worked at the Mount, and a considerable
quantity of ore obtained; any farther excavation,
however, threatened to injure the foundations of
the castle, and it was therefore prudently abandoned.

The remains of the Mine may be seen on the
south side of the hill, and should be visited by
the mineralogist, who will find in the *Drift,** *Tin
crystals* and *Carbonate of Copper*, besides some
other minerals. Veins of Lead are also discover-
able in the rocks. *Mr. Carne* † has lately directed
the attention of the mineralogist to the *veins* of

---

* A *Drift* is a trench or foss, cut in the ground to a certain
depth, resembling a channel dug to convey water to a mill wheel.

† Transactions of the Royal Geological Society of Cornwall,
Vol ii. p. 56.

Mica, which have hitherto only been found in
the granite of this singular spot. They are seldom more than half an inch wide; and, although
tolerably straight, are very short. They generally consist of two layers of Mica in plates,
which meet in the centre of the veins. Some of
the masses of *Granite* which constitute the summit of the Mount have the appearance of an old
wall retaining, in parts, a coating of plaster; this
is the effect of decomposition, and of the *capel*
having in many places remained attached to the
face of the rock, after the vein itself has crumbled
down.

The Botanist will also find some amusement
among the rocks; he will observe the Tamarisk,
(Tamarix Gallica) growing in their crevices, and
relieving by a delicate verdure the harsh uniformity of their surfaces. This shrub was probably
imported from Normandy by the Monks. *Asplenium Marinum* and *Inula Helenium* are also to
be seen among the rocks—but let us leave the
Botanist and Mineralogist to their researches,
while we climb the hill and examine the venerable building on its summit.

We ascend on the north-eastern side by a
rocky winding path, in the course of which,
several remains of its ancient fortifications pre-

sent themselves; thus, about the middle of the
hill, there is a curtain, parallel to, and flanking
the approach, at whose western end is a ravelin,
through which every one is to pass, walled with
three embrasures, and at the angle in the eastern
shoulder is a centry box to guard the passage,
and there was formerly also an iron gate; after
having passed this ruin, we turn to our left, and
ascend by a flight of broken steps to the door of
the castle, whose appearance is much more mo-
nastic than martial. The most ancient parts of
the building are the Entrance, with the Guard-
room on the left hand; the Chapel, and the former Refectory, or common hall of the Monks.
The other parts are of a modern date, although
the style of their architecture confers upon them
a corresponding air of antiquity.

The Refectory, or Common Hall, from the
frieze, with which it is ornamented, appears to
have been fitted up, since the reformation, as a
dining room for a hunting party, and is popularly
denominated " *The Chevy-Chace Room.*" The
cornice represents in stucco, the modes of hunting the wild boar, bull, stag, ostrich, hare, fox,
and rabbit. At the upper end of this room are
the royal arms, with the date 1644; and, at the
opposite end, those of the St. Aubyn family. The

room is 33 feet long, 16 wide, and 18 high, and
has a solemn and imposing appearance, which is
not a little heightened by the antique and appropriate character of its furniture and ornaments.

The Chapel exhibits a venerable monument of
Saxon architecture; its interior has lately been
renewed in a chaste style of elegance, and a
magnificent organ has been erected. During
these repairs, in levelling a platform for the
altar, under the eastern window, a low gothic
door was discovered to have been closed up with
stone in the southern wall, and then concealed
with the raised platform; when the enclosure
was broken through, ten steps appeared descending into a stone vault under the church, about
nine feet long, six or seven broad, and nearly as
many high. In this room was found the skeleton
of a very large man, without any remains of a
coffin. The discovery, of course, gave rise to
many conjectures, but it seems most probable,
that the man had been there immured for some
crime. The bones were removed and buried in
the body of the chapel. At the same time upon
raising the old pavement, the fragment of an
inscribed sepulchral stone of some Prior was
taken up; there was also a grave stone, not inscribed, which Antiquaries have supposed to have

covered the remains of *Sir John Arundel,* of
Trerice, Knight, who was slain on the strand
below, in the wars of York and Lancaster. In
the tower of this chapel are six sweet toned bells,
which frequently ring when *Sir John St. Aubyn*
is resident; at this time also choral service is
performed; and, on a calm day, the undulating
sound of the bells, and the swelling note of the
organ, as heard on the water, produce an effect
which it is impossible to describe.

From the chapel, we may ascend by a narrow
stone stair-case to the top of the tower. The
prospect hence is of the grandest description,
and is perhaps as striking as any that can occur
to " *mortal eye.*" " The immense extent of sea,"
says *Dr. Maton,* " raises the most sublime emo-
tions, the waves of the British, Irish, and Atlantic
seas all roll within the compass of the sight,"
whilst the eye is relieved from the uniform,
though imposing grandeur of so boundless an
horizon, by wandering on the north and west,
over a landscape, which Claude himself might
have transfused on his canvas.

On one of the angles of this tower is to be seen
the carcase of a stone lantern, in which, during
the fishing season, and in dark tempestuous nights,
it may reasonably be supposed that the monks,

to whom the tithe of such fishery belonged, kept a light, as a guide to sailors, and a safeguard to their own property; this lantern is now vulgarly denominated *Saint Michael's Chair*, since it will just admit one person to sit down in it; the attempt is not without danger, for the chair, elevated above the battlements, projects so far over the precipice, that the climber must actually turn the whole body at that altitude, in order to take a seat in it; notwithstanding the danger, however, it is often attempted; indeed one of the first questions generally put to a stranger, if married, after he has visited the Mount,—did you sit in the chair?—for there is a conceit that, if a married woman has sufficient resolution to place herself in it, it will at once invest her with all the regalia of petticoat government; and that if a married man sit in it, he will thereby receive ample powers for the management of his wife. This is probably a remnant of monkish fable, a supposed virtue conferred by some saint, perhaps a legacy of St. Keyne, for the same virtue is attributed to her well.

> " The person of that man or wife,
> Whose chance, or choice attains
> First of this sacred stream to drink,
> Thereby the mastery gains."

On the north-eastern side of the fabric are
situated the modern apartments. They were
erected by the late Sir *John St. Aubyn* upon the
ruins of the ancient convent, in clearing away
which, cart loads of human bones were dug up,
and interred elsewhere, the remains probably
both of the nuns and of the garrison. All that
deserves notice in this part are two handsome
rooms leading into each other, from which the
prospect is of the most extensive description. In
the first parlour, placed in niches, are two large
vases, with an alto relief of statuary marble in
each, relating to Hymeneal happiness.

Let us now take a review of the various interesting events, which the traditionary lore of past
ages represents as having occurred at this spot,
and first of the natural history of the Hill itself.

THE NATURAL HISTORY.—The rock of the
Mount has worn the same aspect for ages; tradition however whispers, that at a remote period
it presented a very different appearance,—that it
was cloathed with wood, and at a considerable
distance from the sea! Its old Cornish name,
" *Carreg Lug en Kug,*" that is, *the hoary rock
in the wood,* would seem to add some probability
to the tradition. It appears also from the original charter of the Confessor, that the Mount was

in his time only *nigh* the sea, for he describes it
expressly as Saint Michael *near* the sea, " Sanct-
um Michaelum qui est *juxta* mare." What this
distance was the charter does not inform us, but
the words of Worcester, who gained his information from the legend of Saint Michael, are sufficiently decisive, " *this place was originally in-
closed within a very thick wood, distant from the
ocean six miles, affording the finest shelter to wild
beasts.*" With respect to the period and causes
of the catastrophe which have changed the face
of this country, we have already offered some
observations.

ECCLESIASTICAL HISTORY.—The Mount appears to have been consecrated by superstition
from the earliest period; and, according to monkish legends, from the supposed appearance of the
archangel Saint Michael to some hermits, upon
one of its craggy points. Tradition has not preserved the place where the vision appeared, but
antiquarianism has attempted to supply the deficiency by conjecture; the spot was denominated
" *Saint Michael's Chair,*" and is said to be one
of the large rocks overhanging the battery, an
appellation which has been erroneously trans-
ferred to the carcase of a stone lantern, situated,
as we have just stated, on the tower of the chapel.

Our poet Milton alludes to this vision in the following passage of his Lycidas—

> " Or whether thou to our moist views deny'd
> " Sleeps't by the fable of Bellerus old
> " *Where the great vision of the guarded Mount*
> " Looks towards Namancos and Bayonas hold.
> " Look homeward Angel now, and melt with ruth,
> " And O ye dolphins, waft the hapless youth."

Spencer also makes mention of this spot in a manner which proves that it was universally hallowed by the devout.

> " In evil hour thou lenst in hond
> " Thus holy hills to blame,
> " For sacred unto Saints they stond,
> " And of them han their name,
> " St. Michael's Mount who does not know
> " That wards the western coast."

Very little is known with respect to the ecclesiastical history of the Mount, previous to its endowment by Edward the Confessor. From what may be collected, however, from expiring tradition, it would appear that so early as the end of the fifth century, Saint Keyne, a holy virgin of the blood royal, daughter of Breganus Prince of Brecknockshire, with her cockle hat and staff, performed a pilgrimage to Saint Michael's Mount : now it is fair to conclude that it was before this time a place universally hallowed, or a person of Saint Keyne's rank would not have paid it such a visit; thus then was it renowned for its sanctity for at least five hundred years before the grant and settlement of it by the Confessor; before this period, however, it was probably little more than an hermitage, or oratory, with the necessary reception for pilgrims.

The Confessor found monks here serving God, and gave them by charter the property of the Mount together with " all the land of *Vennefire* (a district probably in Cornwall), with the towns, houses, fields, meadows, land cultivated, and uncultivated, with their rents; together with a port called *Ruminella* (Romney in Kent), with all things that appertain, as mills and fisheries," first obliging them to conform to the rule of the order of Saint Benedict.

The peculiar respect in which this church was held may be estimated from an instrument recorded by William of Worcester, and asserted to have been found amongst its ancient registers.

" To all members of Holy Mother Church, who
" shall read or hear these letters, Peace and Sal-
" vation. Be it known unto you all, that our
" Most Holy Lord Pope Gregory, in the year of
" Christ's Incarnation, 1070, out of his great zeal
" and devotion to the church of Mount Saint
" Michal, in Tumba, in the county of Cornwall,

E

" hath piously granted to the aforesaid church,
" which is entrusted to the Angelical Ministry,
" and with full approbation, consecrated and
" sanctified, to remit to all the *faithful,* who shall
" *enrich, endow,* or *visit* the said church, a *third*
" *part* of their *Penance,* and that this grant may
" remain for ever unshaken and inviolable, by
" the authority of God the Father, and of the
" Son, and of the Holy Ghost, he forbids all his
" Successors from attempting to make any altera-
" tion against this Decree."

We learn from the same author, that in order
to encrease, as much as possible, the influx of
votaries to the shrine, the above decree was
placed publicly on the gates of the church, and
enjoined to be read in other churches.

When the Normans came in, Robert Earl of
Morton and Cornwall became the patron of this
religious house, erected buildings, and gave some
lands, but from a superior affection for Normandy, he abridged its liberties, and annexed it
to the monastery of *Saint Michael de periculo
Maris,* on the coast of Normandy, to which situation the Mount is said to bear a striking resemblance; from this time, it became only a cell
dependant upon, and subordinate to that foreign
priory. As these Monks were of the reformed

order of Benedictines, and of the Gilbertine kind,
a nunnery was allowed in their vicinity; this
they would make us believe was done with no
other view, than to shew the triumph of faith
over the impulse of sense, but it certainly must
be confessed, to speak even most charitably of it,
that such an union amid the sequestration of soli-
tude, carries a strange appearance with it to our
protestant suspiciousness. The remains of this
convent, we have already said, were removed by
the late proprietor, and the *New Buildings*, as
they are called, erected on their site; from the
appearance of the carved fragments of stone, and
other marks of architectural distinction, found
among the ruins, the Nunnery appears to have
been by far the most costly and magnificent part
of the edifice, the result we presume of *Monkish
gallantry.* Its establishment appears to have terminated at the time Pomeroy surprised it, (an
account of which transaction is recorded under
the military history,) but the Priory continued a
cell to Saint Michael's in Normandy, until that
connection was destroyed, and all the alien prio-
ries were seized in the reign of Edward the
Third.

Henry the Sixth granted this Priory to King's
College, Cambridge, but it was afterwards trans-

ferred by Edward the Fourth to the nunnery of
Sion, Middlesex ; and so it continued until the
general dissolution ; at which period its revenues
were valued at £110 : 12s. per annum, a considerable sum at that time, especially as the number of Monks maintained on the foundation never
exceeded six ; this sum, together with the government of the Mount, which was then a military
post, was bestowed on Hugh Arundel, who was
executed for rebellion in the year 1548. On his
death it was demised to John Milliton of Penger-
sick, Esq., to William his son, and further to
William Harris, Esq. of Hayne in Devonshire,
connected by marriage with the family of Milliton. Queen Elizabeth, by Letters Patent, in the
29th years of her reign, demised it to Arthur
Harris * of Kenegie, Esq. a younger son of the
above William Harris, for life. It is in the
Patent (which recites the former grants to the
Millitons) described as in the note† below. Arthur

---

* Ancestor of William Arundel Harris Arundel, Esq. of Kenegie.

† Firman nrtsm sti michis ad montem in dco nro cornub ac tot
illum scit domu mansional sive capital messuag nrm vocat *Sainte
Michaells Mounte* als dict *the Priorie of Sainte Michalls Mounte* in
dco com nso cornub quondm menastr de Sion in com nro midd
spectan & ptinen habendum & tenendum ad tmnm & pr tmno vite
natural ipsius Arthuri Harris. Reddendo inde annuatim nob
hered & successoribs nris viginti sex libras tres decem solid et
quatuor denar legalis monete Angel." &c.

Harris was about this time appointed Governor
of the Mount, and held that appointment until
his decease in 1628. It was then granted, it is
supposed, in trust for the Earl of Salisbury, from
whom it passed to Francis Bassett, Esq. who
being imprisoned by the usurping powers in the
reign of Charles the First, was obliged in order
to purchase his liberty to part with it to John St.
Aubyn, Esq. in whose family it now remains.
The present Baronet seldom visits it, a circumstance universally regretted, for no gentleman
better understands how to grace the venerable
seat with Knightly dignity and splendor : Sir
John too is a zealous mineralogist, and might by
his presence in Cornwall contribute essentially
to the progress of that science; in one respect
his absence is fortunately supplied by the vigi-
lance of his agents, and every geologist ought to
feel obliged to them, we allude to the care with
which they protect the picturesque and mineralogical beauties of the rocks by opposing the
sacrilegious removal of any part of them.

MILITARY HISTORY.—From the time of King
Edward the Confessor, to the middle of the reign
of Richard the First, the Mount appears to have
been exclusively the sacred nursery of religion;

the earliest transaction of a military nature was
during the captivity of Richard the First, in Ger-
many, when Henry de la Pomeroy, of Berry
Pomeroy in Devonshire, having stabbed a ser-
jeant at arms who came to summon him to appear
for a heavy crime, fled into Cornwall, and cast
himself upon the protection of John, Earl of
that province, who readily supplied him with an
armed force, for he was then aspiring to his bro-
ther's throne; with this, Pomeroy went in dis-
guise to the Mount, and under a pretence of
visiting his sister, who was in the nunnery, gained
admission, and treacherously reduced it to the
service of the said John; upon the return however of the King from imprisonment, he surren-
dered the garrison on mercy, although, despairing
himself of pardon, he soon died, or as some say,
caused himself to be bled to death; after this
event, the Prior and the Monks were restored to
the full possession of their cells, revenues, and
chapel; a small garrison however was still maintained, to defend it against the sudden invasion
of enemies, and in this condition, " manned out
with carnal and spiritual soldiers," did the Mount
remain for a space of 275 years, when another
military transaction occurred to disturb its repose. After the defeat of the Lancastrians at

Barnet, in the eighteenth year of Edward the Fourth, John Vere, Earl of Oxford, one of the most zealous partisans, fled from the field, set sail for Saint Michael's Mount, and having disguised himself, together with a few attendants, in the habits of pilgrims, obtained entrance, massacred the unsuspecting garrison, and seized the fortress, which he valiantly defended for some time against the forces of Edward, but was at length compelled to surrender. Sir John Arundel de Trerice, Sheriff of Cornwall, at the command of the King, marched thither with *posse comitatus* to besiege it, but he fell a victim on the sands, at its base, and lies buried in the chapel.

In King Henry the Seventh's reign, the Lady Catherine Gordon, wife of Perkin Warbeck, the pretended son of Edward the Fourth, remained here for safety, but after the flight of her husband, she was taken prisoner by Giles, Lord Banbury, and carried before that King.

During the Cornish commotion in the reign of Edward the Sixth, many of the superior families fled to the Mount for security, and were besieged by the rebels, who took the plain at the bottom of the rock by assault, at the time of low water, and afterwards the summit, by carrying great trusses of hay before them to obstruct the defendants sight, and deaden their shot. The situation, together with the fears of the women, and the want of food, obliged the besieged to surrender. During the civil contentions in the reign of Charles the First, the fortifications of the Mount were so much increased, that the works were styled " *impregnable and almost inaccessible.*" The Parliament forces, however, under the command of Colonel Hammond, reduced the place, and liberated the Duke of Hamilton, who was there confined; a service which the historians of that period represent as full of danger and difficulty, and this was the last military transaction that occurred upon this romantic spot. Several batteries were erected by government during the late war, to command the western part of the bay, the eastern being too shallow to allow the entrance of large vessels.

We cannot conclude this account of the Mount without observing, that several antiquarians have considered it as the *Ictis* of Diodorus, whither the Greek merchants traded for Cornish Tin; the limits of this work will not allow us to enter upon the discussion, but we beg to refer the curious reader to an ingenious work, published by *Sir Christopher Hawkins,** and to *Dr. Maton's*

---

* See Sir C. Hawkins's Tract on the Tin Trade of the ancients in Cornwall, and on the *Ictis* of Diodorus Siculus.

" Observations on the Western Counties." It is curious, and satisfactory, that these gentlemen should have arrived at the same conclusion upon the subject, and by nearly the same train of reasoning, without any previous communication with each other.

Sancreet.

EXCURSION II.

TO THE LAND's END.—LOGAN ROCK, &c.

―――――

" The Sun beams tremble, and the purple light
Illumes the dark Bolerium;—seat of storms,
High are his granite rocks; his frowning brow
Hangs o'er the smiling ocean. In his caves,
Where sleep the haggard spirits of the storm,
Wild dreary are the schistose rooks around,
Encircled by the waves, where to the breeze
The haggard cormorant shrieks; and far beyond
Are seen the cloud-like islands, grey in mists."

Sir H. Davy.

―――――

In an excursion to the *Land's End* the traveller will meet with several intermediate objects
well worthy his attention, more worthy, perhaps,
than the celebrated promontory itself, as being
monuments of the highest antiquity in the kingdom. They consist of " *Druidical circles, Cairns,*
or circular heaps of stones, *Cromlechs, Crosses,*
Military Entrenchments, and the obscure remains
of *Castles.* Many of these venerable objects,
however, to the eternal disgrace of the inhabi-

tan'ts be it spoken, have of late been much mutilated, and indeed some have been entirely demolished. That the noblest monuments of Greece
should have been converted into lime by the
barbarous Turks, or that the temple of Diana
should have furnished a cement for the volup-
tuous apartments of the Haram, are instances of
degeneracy which we might have been prepared
to witness in such a people; but that the venerable remains of British antiquity, the silent but
faithful monuments of men and days long past,
which are so interesting from their connection
with the primitive history of our island, should
in this enlightened age have been sawed into gate
post, or converted into pig-troughs, is really
past all endurance.—But to proceed.—In riding
from Penzance to the Land's End, which is about
ten miles distant, the first objects to be noticed
are two beautiful villas, well wooded, and adjoining each other, — *Castle Horneck*, the seat
of the Borlase family, and *Rose Hill*, the property of the Rev. Uriah Tonkin. The sea and
land views from these houses are of the most
enchanting description. In viewing the latter
place, the stranger will scarcely believe that the
spot which now exhibits so rich a pastural scene,
was a few years since a deformed and barren

rock! but what cannot gold effect, or where is
the wild which its magic cannot convert into
fairy land? The cost of the gunpowder alone
for blowing up the rocks to facilitate their removal amounted to several hundred pounds.

About a mile farther west, the road passes
another villa, Trereiffe, the ancient seat of the
family of Nicholls, who have been proprietors of
the great tythes of the parish of Madron from the
period of the reformation. It is now the residence of the Rev. Charles Valentine Le Grice,
into whose possession it has passed by marriage.
The scenery about this place is of a very exquisite cast, and, from the richness of the land,
and luxuriance of its productions, it may be
fairly denominated the garden of the Mount's
Bay. After passing through a shady avenue,
from which we catch a delicious peep of the sea
bounded by a grotesque group of rocks, we take
leave of the picturesque, and plunge into a country of a very different aspect and description,—
rough, wild, and unsheltered; never was contrast
more complete or striking, not a tree is seen to
break the extended uniformity of the hills, nor is
there a single object, with the exception of a few
scattered monuments of antiquity, to recommend
it to notice. The agriculturist may, perhaps,

view the district with somewhat different sensations, for the downs are certainly improveable,
and those portions which have been brought into
tillage have amply rewarded the labour of the
adventurer : indeed in several districts cultivation
has even spread to the very brim of the ocean.

The natural product of the high lands is only a
thin turf interspersed with heath, fern and furze,*
and many huge blocks of granite are disseminated
in all directions; this circumstance has materially
impeded the progress of cultivation, for in order
to remove these *boulders* it is necessary to blast
them with gunpowder ; the fragments, however,

---

* This product is carefully collected, and preserved in stacks
by the inhabitants, for the purpose of fuel. It is worthy of remark that the nature of the fuel employed in a country always
imparts a character to its cookery, hence the striking difference
between that of Paris and London; so in Cornwall, the convenience afforded by the furze in the process of Baking, has given
origin to the general use of pies. Every article of food is dressed
in a pie, whence it has become a proverb, that " *the Devil will
not come into Cornwall, for fear of being put into a pie.*" In a
season of scarcity the Attorneys of the county having at the
Quarter Sessions very properly resolved to abstain from every
kind of pastry, an allusion to the above proverb was very happily
introduced into an Epigram, extemporaneously delivered on the
occasion, and which, from its point and humour, deserves to be
recorded—

"If the proverb be true, that the fame of our pies
Prevents us from falling to Satan a prey,
It is clear that *his friends*—the Attorneys,—are wise
In moving such obstacles out of the way."

become useful in their turn, and are employed in
making enclosures, which bear the provincial
name of *hedges*. This stone, commonly called
Growan, is, moreover, wrought into columnar
masses, eight or ten feet long, which are used as
supporters to sheds and outhouses, or gates posts,
and bridges over rivulets. It is also the material
of which common rollers, mill-stones, salting and
pig-troughs are made; in short, few stones are
converted to more various purposes of rural
œconomy, and it accordingly forms an article of
some commercial value. The mode of splitting it
into the required forms is somewhat curious; it
is effected by applying several wedges to holes
cut, or *pooled* as it is termed, in the surface of
the stone at the distance of three or four inches
from each other, according to its size and hardness; the harder the mass, the easier it may be
split into the required form; the softer, the less
regularly it separates. The blocks of granite
employed in the construction of the Waterloo
Bridge over the Thames were procured from the
downs in the vicinity of Penhryn.*

---

* We insert the following facts collected by *Dr. Paris*, from the
first volume of the Transactions of the Royal Geological Society of
Cornwall—" The total quantity of Granite shipped at Falmouth
during the last seven years, amounts to *Forty Thousand Tons*. It
has been employed for building the Docks at Chatham, and the

The Granite of the Land's End district is remarkable for its coarse grain, and the large proportion of its felspar, which, according to the observations of *Dr. Paris*, may be estimated as high as from 70 to 90 per cent. It moreover possesses an earthy texture, which greatly accelerates its decomposition. This circumstance will in some measure account for the unusual fertility of the *growan* soil in the parishes of Saint Burian, Sennen, and Saint Levan. It will moreover explain the theory of a practice, which would otherwise appear absurd, that of actually applying the disintegrated *growan* to certain lands as a manure!

On a closer examination of this Granite, the prismatic crystals of felspar will often be found to exhibit that structure which *Haüy* calls *hemitrope*; more often, they are termed *macles*, and

---

Waterloo Bridge in London. The lands in the vicinity of Penhryn have furnished it; indeed the quantity actually quarried has been considerably greater, for many of the blocks, in consequence of being damaged, have been condemned and sold at a low price to the inhabitants for building, and other purposes. The number of men generally employed in quarrying it is about four hundred; their wages from twelve to eighteen shillings per week, varying with the quantity raised. The lord of the soil receives one half-penny a foot for all that is quarried; the freight during war was as high as 25 shillings per ton, at present it is only 16s. Fourteen cubic feet weigh one ton. The weight of the blocks generally varies from five *cwt.* to seven tons.

are compounded of two crystals intersecting each other at particular angles.

The Botanist as he rides along in the Summer months will observe amongst the gorse (*Ulex*), which is abundant on each side of the road, the parasitical plant *Cuscuta Epithymum*, (called *Epiphany* by the country people,) winding its spiral structure in all directions, and producing from its reddish hue a beautiful contrast.

The farming of this country is in general slovenly, and certainly very far behind any other part of the kingdom, * although it is but just to acknowledge that *Leha*, a farm situated near the Land's End road, forms a pleasing exception to this general remark. The proprietor, John Scobell, Esq. of Nancealverne, has here introduced the *Drill Husbandry of Northumberland*, which would seem to be well adapted to a country so infested with weeds, those hungry invaders of the farmer's property, and usurpers of his soil. The farmers have a peculiar practice, obviously suggested by the inconstancy of the weather, that of putting up their wheat, barley, and other kinds

---

* It is not more than three hundred years since the art of husbandry was first introduced. The lands were formerly all in common, and the inhabitants being wholly engaged in the mines, actually let out their pastures to the graziers of Devon, by whom they were in return supplied with cattle and corn.

of grain, in the field into what are called " *Arish-mows.*" The sheaves are built up into a regular solid cone about twelve feet high ; the beards all turned inwards, and the butt end only exposed to the weather. The whole is finished by an inverted sheaf of reed or corn and tied to the upper rows.

The first objects of antiquity which we have to notice are the stone crosses placed by the roads' side ; some of them still retain their original situation, while others, broken and mutilated, have been converted into the various purposes of rural œconomy. They appear to have been originally designed as guides to direct the pilgrim to the different churches. A few of the more remarkable of them are represented as vignettes in different parts of the present work, from which the reader will become acquainted with their general appearance.

At BOSCAWEN-UN, in a field about a quarter of a mile west of *Leha,* we meet with one of the most ancient British monuments in the kingdom ; " *a Druidical circle,*" as it has been pronounced, consisting of nineteen stones, some of which have fallen, placed in a circle of about twenty-five feet in diameter, having a single one in the centre. There is considerable doubt and obscurity

F

with respect to the origin and intended use of these circles, of which there are many similar examples in Cornwall. *Camden* is inclined to consider them as military trophies, while *Borlase* deems it highly probable that such monuments were of religious institution, and designed originally and principally for the rites of worship ; at the same time he conceives " they might sometimes have been employed as places of council and judgment, and that, whilst any council or decree was pending, the principal persons concerned stood, each by his pillar, and that where a middle stone was erected, as at *Boscawen-Un*, there stood the Prince or General elect." This must certainly be acknowledged as one of the most extraordinary specimens of antiquarian dreaming ever presented to the public.

About half a mile to the right of the high road stands an object of later origin, but not of less interest to the antiquary ; the ruins of a small oratory, or baptistry, dedicated to *Saint Euinus*, and commonly known by the name of *Chapel Euny*. It is situated near a well, whose waters have been long supposed to possess very extraordinary virtues, and to have performed many miraculous cures. There is a similar ruin, which we shall hereafter have occasion to notice at Madron; and it is worthy of remark that these wells do not possess any mineral impregnation; the sick, however, at this very day, repair to them, while the credulous attempt to read the future in the appearance of the bubbles produced in their waters by the dropping in of pins or pebbles. This mode of divining is perhaps one of the most ancient superstitions that have descended to us, and was termed *Hydromancy.* The Castalian fountain, and many others amongst the Grecians, were supposed to be of a prophetic nature; thus, by dipping a fair mirror into a well did the Patræans of Greece receive, as they vainly imagined, some notice of ensuing sickness, or convalescence.

On the summit of the hill above these ruins, are situated the remains of *Caerbran Castle* or Round (that is *Brennus's Castle*) which is thus described by *Borlase.* " It is a circular fortification, consisting first of a deep ditch, fifteen feet wide, edged with stone, through which you pass to the outer *vallum*, which is of earth, fifteen feet high, and was well perfected towards the north-east, but not so towards the west; within this vallum, passing a large ditch about fifteen yards wide, you come to a stone wall, which quite rounded the top of the hill, and seems to

have been of considerable strength, but lies,
now, like a ridge of disorderly stones; the diameter of the whole is ninety paces, and in the
centre of all is a little circle."

There are no less than seven of these *hill castles,* as they are termed, although they might
with more propriety be called strong entrenchments, to be seen at this time within five miles
around Penzance; all so placed on the hills as
to admit of immediate communication with each
other by signal. From several of them we have
views of the North and South Channel, but from
all of them either that of one sea or the other.
Much doubt has arisen concerning their origin.
Mr. Polwhele attributes them to the Irish, while
Dr. Borlase, like an orthodox antiquary, who
takes shelter, whenever he is bewildered, under
the sanction of a popular name, at once boldly
decides upon their Danish origin.

The lonely ruins of *Chapel Carn Bre* next
attract our notice; they are situated upon the
extremity of a high granite ridge, overlooking
the surfy recess of *Whitsand Bay*; from their
great elevation they are visible from every part
of the country, although they scarcely form a
skeleton of the original building, and in a short
time, probably, not a vestige will remain to mark

the consecrated spot. It appears to have been a Chantry, erected for the performance of religious service for the safety of mariners. It is not for the inspection of these ruins that we direct the stranger to ascend the hill, for they are too insignificant to merit attention, but it is for the purpose of his viewing the extensive prospect which its summit commands,—a wild expanse of waters occupying twenty-nine points of the compass!—From this spot also Saint Michael's Mount has a singularly fine effect, appearing as if placed in the centre of a lake at a distance from the ocean.

We now proceed to *Sennan Church-town,* * which according to barometrical admeasurement is 391 feet above the level of the sea. It is about a mile from the *Land's End,* and is celebrated for containing the Ale-house whimsically called " *The First and Last Inn in England.*" On the western side of its sign is inscribed " *The First,*" and on the eastern side " *The Last Inn in England.*"

The last village towards the Land's End is named *Mayon* or *Mean.* In this place is the

---

* *Chnrch-Town.* This expression is peculiar to Cornwall—the fact is, that since many market, and even Borough towns are *without* a church, the Cornish dignify those that have it with the title of *Church-town.*

large stone spoken of by Dr. Borlase under the
name of " *Table mean*," and concerning which
there is a vague tradition that three kings once
dined together on it, in their journey to the
Land's End.

On the turf between this village and the Land's
End, the Botanist will find *Bartsia Viscosa*, and
Illocebrum Verticillatum, the latter of which is
peculiar to this county.

Having arrived at the celebrated Promontory,
we descend a rapid slope, which brings us to a
bold group of rocks, composing the western extremity of our island. Some years ago a military
officer who visited this spot, was rash enough to
descend on horseback; the horse soon became
unruly, plunged, reared, and, fearful to relate,
fell backwards over the precipice, and rolling
from rock to rock was dashed to atoms before it
reached the sea. The rider was for some time
unable to disengage himself, but at length by a
desperate effort he threw himself off, and was
happily caught by some fragments of rock, at
the very brink of the precipice, where he remained suspended in a state of insensibility until
assistance could be afforded him ! The awful
spot is marked by the figure of a horse-shoe,
traced on the turf with a deep incision, which is

cleared out from time to time, in order to preserve it as a monument of rashness which could
be alone equalled by the good fortune with which
it was attended.

Why any promontory in an island should be
exclusively denominated the Land's *End*, it is
difficult to understand; yet so powerful is the
charm of a name, that many persons have visited
it on no other account; the intelligent tourist,
however, will receive a much more substantial
gratification from his visit; the great geological
interest of the spot will afford him an ample
source of entertainment and instruction, while
the magnificence of its convulsed scenery, the
ceaseless roar, and deep intonation of the ocean,
and the wild shrieks of the Cormorant, all com-
bine to awaken the blended sensations of awe
and admiration.

The cliff which bounds this extremity is rather
abrupt than elevated, not being more than sixty
feet above the level of the sea. It is composed
entirely of Granite, the forms of which present a
very extraordinary appearance, assuming in some
places the resemblance of *shafts* that had been
regularly cut with the chisel; in others, regular
equidistant fissures divide the rock into horizontal masses, and give it the character of basaltic

columns; in other places, again, the impetuous waves of the ocean have opened, for their retreat, gigantic arches, through which the angry billows roll and bellow with tremendous fury.

Several of these rocks from their grotesque forms have acquired whimsical appellations, as that of the *Armed Knight*, the *Irish Lady*, &c. An inclining rock on the side of a craggy head-land, south of the Land's End, has obtained the name of *Dr. Johnson's Head*, and visitors after having heard the appellation seldom fail to acknowledge that it bears some resemblance to the physiognomy of that extraordinary man.

On the north, this rocky scene is terminated by a promontory 229 feet above the level of the sea, called " *Cape Cornwall*," between which and the Land's End, the coast retires, and forms *Whitsand Bay*; a name which it derives from the peculiar whiteness of its sand, and amongst which the naturalist will find several rare microscopic shells. There are, besides, some historical recollections which invest this spot with interest. It was in this bay that Stephen landed on his first arrival in England; as did king John, on his return from Ireland; and Perkin Warbeck, in the prosecution of those claims to the crown to which some late writers have been disposed to consider

that he was entitled, as the real son of Edward
the Fourth. In the rocks near the southern ter-
mination of *Whitsand Bay* may be seen the junction of the granite and slate; large veins of the
former may be also observed to traverse the
latter in all directions.

In viewing the whole of the scenery of this
stern coast " it is impossible" says De Luc, not
to be struck with the idea, that *the bed of the sea
is the effect of a vast subsidence,* in which the strata
were broken off on the edge of what, by the retreat of the sea towards the sunken part, became
a *continent*; the many small islands, or rocks of
granite, appear to be the memorials of the land's
abridgement, being evidently parts of the sunken
strata remaining more elevated than the rest."
There is a small *Archipelago* of this kind called
the *Long-ships,* at the distance of two miles west
of the Land's end; on the largest of these rocks
is a light-house, which was erected in consequence of the very dangerous character of the
coast, by a Mr. Smith, in the year 1797, who obtained a grant from the Trinity House, and was
rewarded for a limited number of years by a certain rate on all ships that passed it. This period
having expired, it is at present under the juris-

diction of the Trinity House.* The tower is constructed of granite, the stones of which are *tre-
nailed* on the same plan as that adopted by Smea-
ton in the construction of the Eddystone light-
house. The circumference of the tower at its
base is 68 feet; the height from the rock to the
vane of the lantern, 52 feet; and from the sea to
the base of the light-house it is 60 feet; but not,
withstanding this elevation its lantern has been
often dashed to pieces by the spray of the ocean
during the winter's tempest! The management
of this establishment is entrusted to two men,
who during the winter are often, for two or three
months, confined to this sea-girt prison without
the possibility of communicating with the land;
they accordingly lay in a store of provisions, as
if they were about to embark for a long voyage.

We have already stated that the historians of
Cornwall, from Leland, Norden, and Carew,
downwards, have all recorded the ancient tradition of a considerable portion of the Mount's
bay having been formerly woodland. They have
likewise handed down the concurrent tradition
relative to the supposed tract of land which once

---

* We take this opportunity to state, that the annual revenue of
the Long-ships lighthouse is about three thousand pounds. Every
British vessel that passes pays a halfpenny per ton;—every foreign
vessel pays one shilling, without reference to its tonnage.

connected the islands of Scilly with Cornwall. This tract, to which we are told was given the name of the *Lioness* ("*the Silurian Lyonois,*") is said to have contained one hundred and forty parish churches, all of which were swept away by the resistless ocean! As to the Cornish word *Lethowstow*, or *Lioness*, by which the sea between Scilly and Cornwall is distinguished, we may observe, that the appropriation of such a term is sufficiently accounted for from the general violence and turbulence of the sea, just as the celebrated rock lying south of the channel between the Land's end and Scilly retains the name of the *Wolf*,* from the howling of the waves around it. Those who may wish for farther evidence upon this subject may consult *Mr. Boase's* excellent memoir " On the submersion of part of the Mount's bay," published in the second volume of the Transactions of the Geological Society of Cornwall.

We shall in this place make a short digression, in order to afford some account of the *Scilly Islands*, which are situated in a cluster about nine leagues, west by south, from the Land's end, and are distinctly visible from it.

---

* It is a curious fact that the whole or part of this rock is *Lime* stone.

The SCILLY ISLANDS were called by the
Greeks *Hesperides* and *Capiterides*, or the *Tin
Isles*, and by this name they are mentioned by
Diodorus Siculus, Strabo, and Solinus.   They
must, however, have undergone some material
revolution since the age of these writers, for we
fail in every attempt to reconcile their present
state with the description which they have transmitted to us; and what is very unaccountable,
not a vestige of any ancient mine can be discovered in the islands, except in one part of
Trescow; and these remains are so limited, that
they rather give an idea of an attempt at discovery, than of extensive and permanent mining.   We are strongly inclined to believe that
the Tin of those days came, in part at least, from
the opposite coast of Saint Just, but of this we
shall hereafter speak more fully.   In the time of
Strabo we learn that the number of these Islands
did not exceed *ten*, whereas at present there are
upwards of *one hundred and forty*, but of which
the following only are inhabited, viz. *Saint
Mary's, Saint Agnes', Saint Martin's Trescow,
Bryer*, and *Sampson*. It is curious that the name
of the cluster should have been derived from one
of the smallest of the islets (Scilly), whose surface does not exceed an acre.   The number of

inhabitants amounts to about two thousand, nearly half of which reside in Saint Mary's, which contains 1600 acres; it possesses three towns, a pier, a garrison, a custom house, and some monuments of British antiquity.

At SAINT AGNES is a very high and strong lighthouse, which was erected in the year 1680. Its present machinery was designed by the ingenious Adam Walker, the well known lecturer on Natural Philosophy, although it has lately undergone some modification at the suggestion of Mr. Wyatt. The machinery consists of a triangular frame attached to a perpendicular axis, which, by means of an appropriate power, is made to revolve once every three minutes. On each face of the triangle are arranged ten parabolic reflectors of copper plated with silver, each having an argand lamp in its focus. By this device the light progressively sweeps the whole horizon, and by its regular intermission and increase is readily distinguished from every other on the coast.*

The civil government of these islands is chiefly managed by twelve of the principal inhabitants,

---

* Vessels passing this light pay the same dues as those received by the Long-ships, except in the case of coasting vessels, which pay, not according to their tonnage, but simply a shilling per vessel.

who meet monthly at Heugh Town, St. Mary's, and settle differences by compromise. The Duke of Leeds holds the islands by lease for thirty-one years from the year 1800, at the rent of £40, besides paying the fine of £4000, as a renewal.

The reader is no doubt anxiously waiting to be introduced to the classical descendants of the Grecian or Phœnician race,—Whether they have been swallowed up with the " Lioness," or washed into the ocean by the tempests, we know not; but certain it is that the present inhabitants are all new comers;—Phœnician or Grecian, there are none. —*Jenkins, Ellis, Hicks, Woodcock, Ashford,* and *Gibson** are names which would even defy the ingenious author of the Diversions of Purley to trace to a classical source.

The Scillonians are a robust and healthy people, and were it not for the facility with which they obtain spirits, they would attain a very advanced age. It is a common saying amongst them, and is no doubt intended to express how highly favourable the spot is to longevity, although it obviously admits of another construction, that " *for one man who dies a natural death,*

---

* One half of the inhabitants of St. Agnes are named *Hicks ;* one quarter of those of Trescow, and a third of those at Bryher are called *Jenkins ;* and a half of St. Martin's is divided between *Ellis* and *Ashford.*

nine are drowned." It has been remarked that a
deformed person is not to be found in the islands;
but we apprehend that this fact requires an explanation very different from that which is usually assigned; it cannot be received as any test
of the salubrity of the spot, or of the superior
healthiness of the race; the fact is simply this,
that exposure to inclement weather, want of
proper food, and those various privations which
necessarily increase as we recede from the luxu-
ries of civilization, kill, during infancy, those
feeble subjects which might, otherwise, have
become deformed during the progress of their
growth. It is for the same reason that we so
frequently observe the troops of barbarous countries composed of the most athletic individuals, for
the hardship of their service weeds out the feeble
and invalid. We have already alluded to the
tenacity with which the Cornishman clings to his
native soil, but the attachment of the Scillonian,
if possible, is still stronger to his desolate rock.
What a striking contrast does this form with the
roving inhabitant of an alluvial country, where
every object, it might be presumed, was calculated to excite and sustain the strongest attachment; but this principle of Nature is wise and
universal,—the plant is easily loosened from a

generous soil, but with what difficulty is the lichen torn from its rock.

The islanders are chiefly employed in fishing, making kelp from the *Algæ*, which is disposed of to the Bristol merchant for the use of the glass manufacturer, and in pilotage. From a combination, however, of unfortunate circumstances, in addition to the fatal blow given to the smuggling trade, by the activity of the preventive service, the inhabitants were reduced to such extreme distress that it became necessary in the year 1819 to appeal to the generosity of the public in their behalf; and, notwithstanding the great difficulties of the times, the sum of nine thousand pounds was collected for their relief. In this great work of charity it is but an act of justice to state, that the Society for promoting Christian knowledge, by their purse, as well as by their writings, performed a very essential service. The funds thus obtained were in part appropriated to the relief of the immediate and pressing distress under which they laboured, while the remainder was very judiciously applied towards the promotion of such permanent advantages as might prevent the chance of its recurrence. A Fish-cellar was accordingly provided in the island of Trescow, for the purpose of storing and curing fish ; boats

adapted for the Mackarel and Pilchard Fisheries
were purchased, and others were repaired ; nets
and various kinds of tackling were also at the
same time liberally supplied. By such means
have the inhabitants of these cheerless rocks
been enabled to avail themselves of some of the
resources which Providence has placed within
their reach, and their families have been thus
enabled to exist without the dread of absolute
starvation.* Much, however, still remains for
philanthropic exertion, and should this humble
volume fall into the hands of those, who are
enabled by the superior gifts of fortune to
contribute to the wants of their unhappy breth-
ren, we may perhaps serve their cause by stating that any donation, however small, will be
received by *Henry Boase, Esq.* at the Penzance
Bank. The greatest benefit would arise from the
extension of their fisheries, for in consequence of
the peculiar situation and convenience of these
islands, the Cod and Ling fisheries might be car-

---

* See " A view of the present state of the Scilly Islands; exhibiting their vast importance to the British Empire, the Improvements of which they are susceptible, and a particular account of the
means lately adopted for ameliorating the condition of the Inhabitants, by the establishment and extension of their Fisheries. By the
Rev. George Woodley, Missionary from the Society for promoting
Christian Knowledge; and Minister of St. Agnes, and St. Martin's." *8vo. pp.* 344. *London,* 1822.

ried to almost any extent; and, while boats in any part even of the Mount's Bay, would be weather-bound with the wind W.S.W. to S., they can proceed from Scilly into the channel, without the least difficulty. The Scillonians, however, have as yet been unable to avail themselves of the advantages of their locality; the want of proper boats prevents their proceeding in the pursuit of their occupation, farther than four or five leagues from the land.

During the summer months various species of fish are caught with hook and line; among the smaller kind, which are salted by the Scillonians for their winter consumption, are " *Bass, Wrass, Chad, Scad, Brit, Barne, Cuddle, Whistlers,* &c. all of which are included by the islanders under the general appellation of " *Rock-fish.*"

There is a very curious fact noticed here with respect to the *Woodcock.* These birds generally arrive in Scilly before they are observed in any part of England; more frequently with a north-east,* though sometimes with a north-west wind, and are often so exhausted as to be caught in great numbers by the inhabitants, especially near

---

* The same wind is said to bring them on the Southern shores of Ireland. It is generally believed that they come from Norway, not so much to avoid the cold, as to obtain the worms which are locked up in the earth during the frost.

the lighthouse, the splendour of whose light appears to attract them, and striking against its lantern they not unfrequently fall lifeless in the gallery. It is for the naturalist to consider from whence they migrate.

The Climate of these islands is both milder and more equable than that of Cornwall, but this advantage is counterbalanced by the frequent occurrence of the most sudden and violent storms. By those who have kept journals it has been found that not more than six days of perfect calm occur in the course of a year, and that the wind blows from between S.W. and N.W. for more than half of that period.

With respect to Geology, these islands will afford but little variety; with the exception of some beds of *Porphyry* at Saint Mary's, and some beds of *Chlorite*, containing *Pyrites*, in the same island, they consist entirely of Granite, and are doubtless a continuation of the Devonian range, although the rock assumes an appearance less porphyritic; it contains, however, veins of red Granite. At the Lizard Point in the island of Trescow, a variety of granite occurs, in which the felspar is of a remarkably pure white, and might, we should conceive, be advantageously employed in the manufacture of Porcelain. In some chasms of this rock, and in the centre of large masses, the *Mica* is of a silvery hue, and occurs crystallized in its primitive form. In the same island is a remarkable cavern, in the centre of which is a pool of fresh water. The porphyritic beds in Saint Mary's are interesting on account of the distinct appearance of stratification which they display, and *Mr. Majendie* thinks that an undoubted instance of stratified granite is to be seen near the same spot. The Granite of Scilly is very liable to decomposition; whence has arisen all that fancied statuary of the Druids, of which we have spoken in another place. The Islands are undoubtedly undergoing a gradual diminution. At no great distance of time Saint Mary's will probably be divided by the sea, and a channel formed through the low land between the New-town and the south-east side of the garrison. This might perhaps be prevented by throwing down masses of granite from a neighbouring hill, so as to form a barrier against the sea. The object may be worthy of attention, as the sea in winter, with a high tide, has been known to pass over this land, and the effect of its forcing a channel there would be to divide the garrison from the rest of the island. If the Geologist proceeds to a spot behind the quay, and be-

tween the front of the garrison-hill and that
island, he will be gratified by the discovery of a
process the very converse of that which we have
been just describing. In these places the granitic
sand is becoming indurated by the slow infiltra-
tion of water holding iron in solution, and which
appears to be derived from the decomposing hills
above it. Some fine specimens of this " *regene-
rated*" granite have been placed in the Geological Society's cabinet at Penzance.

We now return to the Land's End,—from
which we should proceed to visit a promontory
called " *Castle Treryn*," where is situated the
celebrated " *Logan Stone*." If we pursue our
route along the cliffs, it will be found to lie several miles south-east of the Land's End, although
by taking the direct and usual road across the
country, it is not more than two miles distant;
but the Geologist must walk, or ride along the
coast on horseback, and we can assure him that
he will be amply recompensed for his trouble.

From the Cape on which the signal station is
situated, the rock scenery is particularly magnificent, exhibiting an admirable specimen of the
manner, and forms, into which Granite disintegrates. About forty yards from this Cape is the
promontory called *Tol-Pedn-Penwith*, which in

the Cornish language signifies the *holed headland
in Penwith*. The name is derived from a singular chasm, known by the appellation of the *Fun-
nel Rock*; it is a vast perpendicular excavation
in the granite, resembling in figure an inverted
cone, and has been evidently produced by the
gradual decomposition of one of those vertical
veins with which this part of the coast is so frequently intersected. By a circuitous route you
may descend to the bottom of the cavern, into
which the sea flows at high water. Here the
Cornish Chough *(Corvus Graculus)* has built its
nest for several years, a bird which is very common about the rocky parts of this coast, and may
be distinguished by its red legs and bill, and the
violaceous blackness of its feathers. This promontory forms the Western extremity of the
Mount's Bay. The antiquary will discover in
this spot the vestiges of one of the ancient " *Cliff
Castles*," which were little else than stone walls,
stretching across necks of land from cliff to cliff.
The only geological phenomenon worthy of particular notice is a large and beautiful contemporaneous vein of *red Granite* containing *Shorl*; is
one foot in width, and may be seen for about
forty feet in length.

Continuing our route around the coast we at

length arrive at "*Castle Treryn.*" Its name is
derived from the supposition of its having been
the site of an ancient British fortress, of which
there are still some obscure traces, although the
wild and rugged appearance of the rocks indicate
nothing like art.

The foundation of the whole is a stupendous
group of Granite rocks, which rise in pyramidal
clusters to a prodigious altitude, and overhang
the sea. On one of those pyramids is situated
the celebrated "*Logan Stone,*" which is an
immense block of Granite weighing above 60
tons. The surface in contact with the under
rock is of very small extent, and the whole mass

is so nicely balanced, that, notwithstanding its
magnitude, the strength of a single man applied
to its under edge is sufficient to change its centre
of gravity, and though at first in a degree scarcely
perceptible, yet the repetition of such impulses,
at each return of the stone, produces at length a
very sensible oscillation! As soon as the astonishment which this phenomenon excites has in some
measure subsided, the stranger anxiously en-
quires how, and whence the stone originated—
was it elevated by human means, or was it produced by the agency of natural causes?—Those
who are in the habit of viewing mountain masses
with geological eyes, will readily discover that
the only chisel ever employed has been the tooth
of time—the only artist engaged, the elements.
Granite usually disintegrates into rhomboidal
and tabular masses, which by the farther operation of air and moisture gradually lose their solid
angles, and approach the spheroidal form. *De
Luc* observed, in the Giant mountains of Silesia,
spheroids of this description so piled upon each
other as to resemble Dutch cheeses; and appearances, no less illustrative of the phenomenon,
may be seen from the signal station to which we
have just alluded. The fact of the upper part
of the cliff being more exposed to atmospheric

agency, than the parts beneath, will sufficiently explain why these rounded masses so frequently rest on blocks which still preserve the tabular form; and since such spheroidal blocks must obviously rest in that position in which their lesser axes are perpendicular to the horizon, it is equally evident that whenever an adequate force is applied they must vibrate on their point of support.

Although we are thus led to deny the Druidical *origin* of this stone, for which so maay zealous antiquaries have contended, still we by no means intend to deny that the Druids employed it as an engine of superstition; it is indeed very probable that, having observed so uncommon a property, they dexterously contrived to make it answer the purposes of an ordeal, and by regarding it as the *touchstone* of truth, acquitted or condemned the accused by its motions. Mason poetically alludes to this supposed property in the following lines.

> " Behold yon huge
> And unknown sphere of living adamant,
> Which, pois'd by magic, rests its central weight
> On yonder pointed rock: firm as it seems,
> Such is its strange, and virtuous property,
> It moves obsequious to the gentlest touch
> Of him, whose heart is pure, but to a traitor,
> Tho' e'en a giant's prowess nerv'd his arm,
> It stands as fix'd as Snowdon."

The rocks are covered with a species of *Byssus*

long and rough to the touch, forming a kind of
hoary beard; in many places they are deeply
furrowed, carrying with them a singular air of
antiquity, which combines with the whole of the
romantic scenery to awaken in the minds of
the poet and enthusiast the recollection of the
Druidical ages. The Botanist will observe the
common Thrift *(Statice Armeria)* imparting a
glowing tinge to the scanty vegetation of the spot,
and, by growing within the crevices of the rocks,
affording a very picturesque contrast to their
massive fabric. Here too the *Daucus Maritimus,*
or wild carrot; *Sedum Telephium,* *Saxifraga
Stellaris,* and *Asplenium Marinum,* may be found
in abundance.

The Granite in this spot is extremely beautiful, on account of its porphyritic appearance;
the crystals of felspar are numerous and distinct;
in some places the rock is traversed by veins of
red felspar, and of black tourmaline, or schorl,
of which the crystalline forms of the prisms, on
account of their close aggregation, are very in-
distinct. Here may also be observed a contemporaneous vein of *schorl rock* in the granite,
nearly two feet wide, highly inclined and very
short, and not having any distinct walls. On
the western side of the Logan rock is a cavern,

formed by the decomposition of a vein of granite, the felspar of which assumes a brilliant flesh-red, and lilac colour; and, where it is polished by the sea, exceeding even in beauty the *Serpentine caverns* at the Lizard.

Mr. Majendie observed in this spot numerous veins of fine grained granite, which he is inclined to consider as *cotemporaneous*; he also observed what, at first sight, appeared to be fragments, but which, upon closer examination, he pronounces to be *cotemporaneous concretions*; for large crystals of *felspar* may be seen shooting from the porphyritic granite into these apparent fragments. These phenomena are extremely interesting in a geological point of view, and well deserve the attention of the scientific tourist.

In Treryn cove, just below the site of the castle, Dr. Maton found several of the rarer species of shells, as *Patella Pellucida, P. Fissura, Mytilus Modiolus, Trochus Conulus, Turbo Cimex,* and *T. Fascitatus* (of Pennant.)

Before we quit this coast we beg to state, for the information of the geological tourist, that the *Granite* which we have just traced from beyond the Land's End to this spot, continues until within half a mile of the signal post near Lemorna cove, where it meets with a patch of slate, and is

lost for about the space of three quarters of a
mile. At the western extremity of this junction
(*Carn Silver*) the mineralogist will find embedded Garnet-rock with veins of *Epidote* and
Axinite. Here may also be seen the rare occurrence of a granite vein penetrating both the slate
and the granitic rock.

But let us return.——About two miles north-
east of the Logan rock, and in the high road to
Penzance, stands the town of SAINT BURYAN,
which though now only a group of wretched cottages was once a place of very considerable note,
and the seat of a College of Augustine Canons;
the latter was founded by Athelstan after his
return from the conquest of the Scillÿ Islands,
A.D. 930. The remains of the College were wan-
tonly demolished by one Shrubshall, Governor
of Pendennis Castle, during the usurpation of
Cromwell.

The Church tower stands on the highest point
in this part of the country, being 467 feet above
the level of the sea ; it consequently forms a very
conspicuous object, and is so exposed to the rains
from the Atlantic, that the stones carry a decep-
tive face of freshness with them which lends an
aspect of newness to the whole building. From
the top of the tower the prospect is of a very

extensive kind, commanding the whole range of the surrounding country, and an immense surface of sea. In clear weather the Scilly Islands may be easily distinguished in the horizon, especially with a setting sun, when they appear to project from the brilliant ground of the western sky like figures embossed on burnished gold.

Both from the history and appearance of this edifice the antiquary will enter it with sensations of awe and veneration, but he will find with regret that the ancient Roodloft has been lately removed, from an idea that it deadened the voice of the preacher, and that the parishioners have also converted the original forms into modern pews, a change which has cruelly violated the venerable uniformity of the interior. There is a singular monument in the church, in the shape of a coffin, having an inscription around the border in very rude characters, and now partly obliterated; it is in Norman French, and has been thus translated.

CLARICE

The wife of Geffrei de Bollait lies here
God of her soul have mercy
They who pray for her soul shall have
Ten days Pardon.

On the middle of the stone is represented a Cross fleury, standing on four steps; the monument is said to have been found many years ago by the sexton, while sinking a grave.

Opposite the great door in the church-yard stands a very ancient Cross, on one side of which are five balls, and, on the other, a rude figure intended to represent the crucified Saviour. We here present our readers with a sketch of this singular monument.

Buryan Church-yard.

Another Cross stands in the road, and faces the entrance into the church-yard, of which also we have introduced a delineation.

Buryan.

The Deanery is in the gift of the Crown, as a royal peculiar, and is tenable with any other preferment. The Dean exercises an independent jurisdiction in all ecclesiastical matters within the parish of St. Burian, and its dependent parishes of St. Levan, and Sennan. He is the Rector, and is entitled to all tithes. A Visitation court is held in his name, and the appeal from it is only to the King in council. Athelstan is said to have granted to this church the privilege of a Sanctuary, and a ruin overgrown with ivy; standing on an estate called *Bosliven,* about a mile east from the church, is thought to be its remains, but Mr. Lysons justly observes that the *Sanctuary* usually comprised the church itself, and perhaps a certain privileged space beyond it, and that the ruins to which the tradition attaches, are probably those only of an ancient chapel.

From St. Buryan the traveller may at once return to Penzance, which is about six miles distant, but as no object of particular interest will occur in the direct road, it is unnecessary for us to attend him thither. Should he, however, be inclined to extend his excursion, he will receive much gratification in returning by a somewhat circuitous route along the southern coast, through the parish of Saint Paul. In this case, we may

first proceed to *Boskenna,* the seat of John
Paynter Esq. a highly romantic spot, abounding
with woodcocks, and which under the direction
of a skilful landscape gardener might be made to
emulate in beauty any of the charming villas that
adorn the under-cliff of the Isle of Wight. On
this estate there is a superficial quarry of decomposing granite, which the mineralogist ought to
visit, for the purpose of obtaining some remarkably fine specimens of felspar in separate crystals, which may be easily removed from the mass
in which they lie imbedded.

At *Bolleit,* in a croft near Boskenna, and adjoining the high road, is to be seen a circle of
stones very similar to that we have already described (p. 81,) except that it has not a central
pillar; the appellation given to these stones is
that of the " *Merry Maidens,*" on account of a
whimsical tradition, that they were once young
women transformed like Niobe into stones, as
a punishment for the crime of dancing on the
Sabbath day. In a field on the opposite side of
the road there are two upright stones standing
about a furlong asunder, the one being nearly
twelve, the other sixteen feet in height. They
are probably sepulchral monuments; the same
ridiculous tradition, however, attaches to them

as to the circle, and has accordingly bestowed upon them the appellation of the " *Pipers.*"

At Carn Boscawen, on this coast, is to be seen a very extraordinary group of rocks, consisting of a large flat stone, the ends of which are so poised upon the neighbouring rocks, as to leave an opening underneath; *Dr. Borlase,* with his accustomed zeal, insists upon its Druidical origin, and ever ready to supply the deficiency of both history and tradition by the sallies of an active imagination, very confidently informs us, that " this said opening beneath the pensile stone was designed for the seat of some considerable person, from which he might give out his edicts, and decisions, his predictions, and admissions to Noviciates"!—*Risum teneatis geologici?*

In our road to Saint Paul, we pass *Trouve,* or *Trewoof,* an estate situated on the side of a woody hill, overlooking a romantic valley, which is terminated by *Lemorna Cove,* a spot which should be visited by every stranger who delights in the " lone majesty of untamed Nature." Within the estate of Trouve are the remains of a triple entrenchment, in which runs a subterranean passage; and, it is said, that during the civil wars a party of Royalists were here concealed from the observation of the forces of Sir Thomas

Fairfax. There is a fine chalybeate spring on this estate.

At KERRIS, in the parish of Paul, about five miles from Penzance, is an oval enclosure called " *Roundago*," which is stated to have been connected with Druidical rites; time and the Goths, however, have nearly destroyed its last remains, so that the antiquary will require the eyes of a Borlase to recognise its existence by any description hitherto given of it.

PAUL CHURCH is a very conspicuous object from its high elevation,* and interests the historian from the tradition, already stated, of its having been burnt by the Spaniards, upon which occasion the south porch alone is said, in consequence of the direction of the wind, to have escaped the conflagration. A pleasing confirmation of this tradition was lately afforded during some repairs, when one of the wooden supporters was found charred at the end nearest the body of the church. It also deserves notice that the thick stone division at the back of the *Trewarveneth* pew, which has so frequently occasioned enquiry, is a part of the old church, which escaped the

---

* It may be observed in the engraving of Saint Michael's Mount, on the elevated line of coast which forms the back ground to the picture.

fire. In the church is the following curious notice of its having been burnt, " *The Spanger
burnt this church in the year* 1595."

Most tourists inform us that in this church-
yard is to be seen the monumental stone, with
the epitaph of *Old Dolly Pentreath,* so celebrated
among antiquaries, as having been the last person who spoke the Cornish language. Such a
monument, however, if it ever existed, is no
longer to be found, nor can any information be
obtained with regard to its probable locality.
Her Epitaph is said to have been both in the
Cornish and English language, viz.

> " Coth Dol Pentreath canz ha deaw
> Marir en Bedans en Powl pleu
> Na en an Eglar ganna Poble braz
> Bet en Eglar Hay Coth Dolly es ! "

> " Old Dol Pentreath, one hundred age and two
> Both born, and in Paul Parish buried too ;
> Not in the Church 'mongst people great and high
> But in the Church-yard doth old Dolly lie ! "

In the parishes of Paul and Buryan are sevesal
Tin streams ; in some of which the *Wood Tin,* or
wood-like oxide of Tin, is occasionally found in
large, and well defined pieces. It has been also,
although rarely, found in its matrix.

From Paul Church we may proceed to Pen-

zance, either by the high road over Paul Hill,
which becomes extremely interesting from the
picturesque beauty and superior cultivation of
the country; or we may descend towards the sea
shore, and return through the villages of *Mousehole* and *Newlyn*, which may be called colonies
of Fishermen, for here the Pilchard * and Mackarel fisheries are carried on to a very great extent; and every kind of fish which frequent this
coast are caught and sent to Penzance, and other
Cornish towns; and, in the early part of the
season, they supply the London market with
Mackarel, which are conveyed thither by way of
Portsmouth. The Lobster fishery also proves
an ample source of revenue to the Mount's Bay
fishermen, from which alone they divide not less
than Two Thousand Pounds, annually.

The ride or walk along the coast from MOUSE-
HOLE to NEWLYN is highly interesting. The
former town which is situated about two miles
south-west of Penzance; and half a mile from
Paul Church-town, contains about six hundred
inhabitants. There is a small Pier capable of
admitting vessels of one hundred tons burthen;
but it is chiefly used as a harbour for the numerous fishing boats.

---

* A History of the Pilchard Fishery will be presented to our
readers in the Excursion to Saint Ives.

NEWLYN, with respect to population, exceeds by one-third that of Mousehole. It has a commodious pier, which is also usually occupied by the fishing boats of the place, which exceed four hundred in number. In the cliff-road between these villages, we pass a platform, which during the late war was a *battery*, forming a security to the bay from any privateers that might visit it. Adjoining this battery stands a furnace for the purpose of heating the shot. It was under the direction of a small party of the Royal Artillery.

The Geologist in performing this part of the excursion will have much to observe. About one hundred yards west of Mousehole, the clay-slate ceases, and the granite commences. At this junction numerous granite veins, varying in width from about a foot to less than an inch, pass through the slate.* A little farther west, a cavern may be observed in the cliff, which has evidently been produced by the decomposition of the walls of an old *Adit*. In this cavern the Mineralogist has found good specimens of *Eisenkeisel*, or Iron flint :——but we will conclude, for our tourist must be wearied by the length of the excursion ;

---

* See *Mr. Majendie's* interesting account of this phenomenon in the first volume of the Royal Geological Society of Cornwall.

tomorrow we shall be again prepared to accompany him in a different direction, and to point out a succession of fresh objects, when antiquities, minerals, and picturesque views will, in their turn, again present themselves for his examination.

Between Penzance, and Buryan.

EXCURSION III.

TO BOTALLACK MINE; CAPE CORNWALL; AND THE
MINING DISTRICT OF SAINT JUST.

———

To exhibit the greatest variety of interesting
objects, in the least possible space and time, may
be said to constitute the essential excellence of a
" *Guide.*" For the accomplishment of such a
purpose we now proceed to conduct the stranger
to *Botallack Mine* and *Cape Cornwall,* through
the Parishes of Madron, Morvah, and Saint Just.

In our road to the village of Madron, or
Madron *Church-town,* as it is commonly called,
we pass *Nancealverne,* the estate of John Scobell
Esq., *Poltair,* the residence of Edward Scobell
Esq., and *Trengwainton* the seat of Sir Rose
Price, Bart. At this latter place considerable
exertions have been made to raise plantations,
and to clothe the granitic hills behind it with
wood; and from the progress already made, we
feel sanguine in the ultimate success of the enter-

prize. Amongst the pictures in the possession of
the worthy Baronet are several of the earlier
productions of Opie. The head of an aged beggar, by that artist, has frequently excited our
admiration, and presents a characteristic specimen
of the native simplicity and expression of his
style, and the magic force of his chiaro-scuro.
This head was painted also under circumstances,
a knowledge of which cannot fail to heighten its
interest. The father of Sir Rose having been
struck by the venerable aspect of an aged mendi-
cant as he was begging in the streets of Penzance,
immediately sent for Opie, then residing in the
town, and expressed a desire that the young
artist should paint his portrait. The beggar was
accordingly regaled with a bounteous meal upon
the occasion, and Opie appears to have caught
his expression at the happy moment, when like
the " Last Minstrel" of our northern bard,

> —— " Kindness had his wants supplied
> And the old man was gratified."

The Village of Madron is about two miles to
the north-west of Penzance. The church is
placed on an elevated situation, and commands
a very striking view of Saint Michael's Mount,
and its bay. Penzance is a Chapelry of this
parish.

MADRON WELL is situated in a moor about a mile and a half from the *Church-town.* It is enclosed within walls, which were partially destroyed in the time of Cromwell, by Major Ceeley of St. Ives, but the remains of them are still sufficiently entire to exhibit the form of an ancient Baptistry. * The inner wall with its window and door-way, and the altar with a square hole or socket in the centre, which received the foot of the cross or image of the patron saint, are still perfect. The foundation of the outer wall, or anti-room, may be traced with great ease.

Superstition has, of course, attributed many virtues to waters which had been thus hallowed, and this Well, like that of Chapel Euny, has been long celebrated for its medicinal efficacy in restoring motion and activity to cripples. † Baptism was administered only at the stated times of Easter and Whitsuntide; but, at all seasons, the virtues of the waters attracted the lame and the impotent; and the altar was at hand to assist the devotion of their prayers, as well as to receive the offerings of their gratitude.

---

* Baptistries were continued out of the church until the sixth century.

† The learned Bishop Hall in his work entitled " *The Mystery of Godliness,*" bears ample testimony to the medicinal efficacy of this water in restoring motion and activity to cripples.

Chemical analysis has been unable to detect in this water the presence of *any* active ingredient that might explain the beneficial operation attributed to it.

In the road to Morvah we meet with the celebrated *Cromlech* * at Lanyon. It is placed on a prominent hill, and from its lonely situation, and the wildness of the country by which it is surrounded, it cannot fail to inspire sensations of reverential awe in every one who approaches it. † This rude monument has been long known amongst the country people by the appellation of the " *Giant's Quoit.*" When the last edition of this " *Guide*" went to the press it was still standing in its original position, and was thus described. It consists of three unshapen pillars

---

* *Cromlech* in the Cornish language signified a crooked stone.

† This ancient monument is faithfully depicted in the frontispiece of the present work; but we are in candour bound to acknowledge that, in the introduction of Saint Michael's Mount, the artist has availed himself of the " *quidlibet audendi*" so universally conceded to Painters and Poets; in reality, an intervening eminence obstructs the view of the Mount from this spot, and he has therefore, upon the present occasion, just taken the liberty to remove this barrier to our vision. If the Geological tourist condemn this harmless deviation from truth, we shall recriminate by reminding him that even Geologists have sometimes appropriated to themselves an indulgence which Horace extended only to the votaries of the Muses, and have not hesitated to overlook the existence of a mountain where it stood in the way of a favourite theory.

inclining from the perpendicular, which support a large table stone (resembling a *Discus* or *Quoit*) in a horizontal position, the direction of which is nearly north and south. The flat stone is 47 feet in girth, and 12 in length, and its height from the ground is sufficient to enable a man on horseback to pass under it.—The aged monument, however, has at length bent beneath the hand of time, and fallen on its side. Its downfall, which happened during a violent tempest, occasioned a universal feeling of regret in the country.

In the same tenement, about a quarter of a mile west of Lanyon house, is another monument of this kind, nearly as large as the former; and it is singular that this should have been the only Cromlech in Corwall which escaped the notice of Dr. Borlase. It has fallen on its edge, but is still entire.

All our notions respecting the origin and use of these monuments are purely conjectural; it seems, however, very probable that they are the most ancient in the world, erected possibly by one of the first colonists which came into the island. As Cromlechs are known to abound in every country where the *Cells* established themselves, many antiquaries have concluded that

they are of Celtic origin. The same doubt and
uncertainty involve every consideration with respect to their use; it has been a general idea
that they were intended for altars, but the upper
stone is evidently too gibbous ever to have admitted the officiating priest, or to have allowed
him to stand to overlook the fire, and the consumption of the victim; besides, what occasion
is there to suppose a Cromlech any thing more
than a sepulchral monument? Is it not the most
natural and probable conclusion? Indeed Mr.
Wright actually found a skeleton deposited under one of them in Ireland, and it must strike
the most superficial observer that our modern
tombs are not very dissimilar to the former in
their construction, and probably derived their
form from a very ancient model.

Men-an-Tol. The next object of curiosity
consists of three stones on a triangular plane,
the middle one of which is perforated with a large
hole, and is called *Men-an-Tol,* i. e. the *holed
stone.* Dr. Borlase who, as we have often observed, has recourse to the chisel of Druidism to
account for every cavity or crevice, conjectures
that it was appropriated to the rites of that
priesthood, and asserts, on the authority of a
farmer, that even in his time, it was deemed to

possess the power of healing those who would crawl through it.

In a croft, about half a mile to the north-west of Lanyon, lies a very ancient sepulchral stone, called by the Cornish " *Men Skryfa,*" i. e. the *Inscribed Stone.* It is nine feet ten inches long, and one foot eight inches broad; the inscription upon it is " *Riolobran Cunoval Fil,*" which signifies *Riolobran the Son of Cunoval lies buried here.** With respect to the date of this monument, all antiquaries agree in thinking that it must have been engraven before the corruptions crept into the Roman alphabet, such for instance as the junction of the letters by unnatural links, or when the down strokes of one were made to serve for two, &c. This practice arose soon after the Romans went off, and increased until the Saxon letters were introduced at Athelstan's conquest. The most striking deviation from the Roman orthography to be observed in this monument is in the cross stroke of the Roman N not being diagonal as it ought to be, nor yet quite horizontal as we find it in the sixth century; and hence

---

* Before the beginning of the seventh century we are informed by Strutt that it was held unlawful to bury tne dead in the cities, and that there were no church-yards. *Anglo-Saxon Æra, vol.* 1. *p.* 69.

it is fair to assign to it a date antecedent to that period.*

CHUN CASTLE, a prominent object in this neighbourhood, is similar to *Caerbran Round,* which has been described, except that the ruins are more extensive, and less confused. The remains occupy the whole area of a hill commanding a wide tract of country to the east, some low grounds to the north and south, and the wide expanded ocean to the west. Another Cromlech may also be seen from this spot, and stands upon the very line which divides the parishes of Morvah and Saint Just; but it is far inferior to that at Lanyon. We will now for awhile abandon the contemplation of these faded monuments of past ages, and proceed to the examination of a rich and interesting field of mineralogical and geological research. In introducing the stranger, however, to the district of Saint Just, we must repeat to him the caution with which Mr. Carne†

---

* There are several monumental inscriptions of the same kind to be seen in Cornwall, but none so ancient as *Men Skryfa.* In Barlowena bottom, for instance, as you pass from the church of Gulval to that of Madron, there is one which is now converted into a foot-bridge across a brook; if the antiquary examine the letters upon this stone, which he cannot conveniently do without getting under it, he will discover the corruptions alluded to in the text, viz. the *I* in *Filius* linked to the *L.*

† To the elaborate memoir, by *Mr. Carne,* published in the second volume of the Transactions of the Royal Geological Society

has very prudently accompanied his history of its mineral productions. " If the stranger on his arrival shall expect to find any of the minerals so prominently situated as to salute his eyes at once; or if he shall suppose that those objects which are especially worthy of notice in a geological point of view, are to be discovered and examined in the space of a few hours, he will be greatly mistaken and disppointed ; for very few, either of the minerals or the veins are to be found *in situ,* except by a diligent, patient, and persevering search.''

Without further delay we shall now attend the traveller to *Pendeen Cove*; in our road to which, the only objects worthy attention are the Stamping Mills, and Burning Houses or Roasting Furnaces, belonging to *Botallack* Mine. They are situated on the bank of the river which runs into the sea at *Pendeen Cove.* The Tin ore of *Botallack* is generally mixed with a portion of *Sulphuret of Copper,* which not being separable from it by the mechanical process of dressing, is submitted to the action of a roasting furnace, by which the Copper being converted into an oxide,

---

of Cornwall, and entitled " *On the Mineral Productions, and the Geology of the Parish of Saint Just,*" we would especially direct the attention of the scientific traveller.

and the Sulphur into Sulphuric acid, a *Sulphate
of Copper* is thus produced, which is easily separated by washing. The solution obtained is then
poured into casks, containing pieces of iron, by
the agency of which the *Copper* is *precipitated.**

There is to be seen at *Pendeen,* a cave, known
by the name of *Pendeen Vau,* and concerning
which there are many ridiculous stories. It appears to have been one of those hiding places in
which the Britons secreted themselves, and their
property, from the attacks of the Saxons and
Danes. The cave is still almost entire, a circumstance which is principally owing to the superstitious fears of the inhabitants, many of whom,
at this very day, entertain a dread of entering it.

At *Pendeen Cove,* the Geologist will meet with
several phenomena well worthy his attention.
At the junction of the Slate and Granite, veins
of the latter will be observed traversing the former rock, and what is particularly worthy of
notice, they may he seen emanating from a great
mass of granite and passing into the schistose rock
by which it is covered. One part of the cliff of

---

* The quantity of Copper procured in this way at Botallack,
says Mr. Carne, is about a ton in a year. This chemical process is
now practised in most of the mines in which the " *Tin-stone*" is
mixed with Copper ore, as in Dolcoath, Cook's Kitchen, Chacewater, and in some parts of St. Agnes.

this cove consists of large fragments of granite imbedded in clay and earth; the interstices of which are filled with white sand, which has been probably blown there from the beach; through this sand, water impregnated with iron is slowly percolating, the effect of which is the induration of the sand, and the formation of a *breccia*, which in some parts has acquired very considerable hardness.

Before proceeding to the metalliferous district of Saint Just, we may observe that, if the traveller's object be to reach Saint Ives by the road along the cliffs, through the parish of *Zennor*, he will meet with a most cheerless country, but by no means destitute of geological interest. He ought particularly to examine a bold rocky promontory, called the " *Gurnard's Head,*" where he will find a succession of beds of slaty felspar, hornblende rock, and greenstone. The geology of this headland has been accurately described by *Dr. Forbes* in the second volume of the *Transactions of the Royal Geological Society of Cornwall.* *Polmear Cove* ought also to be visited on account of the Granite veins, which are perhaps as singular and interesting as any of those already described.—But let us proceed to complete our examination of the coast of *Saint Just.* Many of

I

the mines are situated on the very edge of the
cliff, and are wrought to a considerable distance
under the sea ; but all communication to them
is from land.* For a description of the numerous minerals found in this district,† we must
refer the reader to the highly valuable paper by
Joseph Carne, Esq. which is published in the
second volume of the *Transactions of the Royal
Geological Society of Cornwall.* We cannot, however, allow the mineralogist to pass *Trewellard,*
without reminding him that, at this spot, *Axinite*
was first discovered in Cornwall, and that the
most beautifully crystallized specimens of that
mineral, scarcely inferior to those brought from
Dauphiné, may still be procured here. In the
cliff at *Huel Cock Carn,* a vein of this mineral,
of a violet colour, three feet in width, may be
traced for upwards of twenty yards ; and in its
vicinity there is to be found also a vein of *garnet
rock.* *Apatite,* of a greyish-white colour, associated with *Hornblende,* may be seen in the same
spot. In the slate rocks between *Huel Cock* and

---

* The principal sub-marine mines on this part of the coast are
Levant; Tolvaen; Huel Cock ; and *Huel Castle;* Copper Mines ;
and *Praze; Little Bounds ; Riblose ; Huel St. Just;* Tin Mines ;
and *Botallack* Tin and Copper Mine.

† A miner of the name of *James Wall,* who resides in the village
of *Carnyorth,* has generally a variety of these minerals for sale.

Botallack, *Prehnite* has lately been found, for
the first time; it appears to form a small vein,
which in one part is divided into two branches.
Upon the discovery of the above mineral, says
Mr. Joseph Carne, an expectation was naturally
formed, that *Zeolite*, its frequent associate, and
an equal stranger to Cornwall, might shortly
make its appearance. This opinion has been
lately verified by the discovery of, at least, two
varieties of that mineral, imbedded in the *Prehnite*
vein, viz. *Stilbite*, or *foliated Zeolite*, crystallized
in flat four-sided prisms, with quadrangular summits; and the *radiated Mesotype*, which sometimes contains nodules of *Prehnite*. Other specimens have been found in rather an earthy state,
and may possibly be the *mealy Zeolite* of Jameson.
In the same slate rocks *Apatite* occurs of a yel-
lowish-green colour, and crystallized in hexaedral
prisms. In the granite rocks on the high hills
south-east of Trewellard, *Pinite* is to be observed.

We arrive at the " *Crown Engine*" of Botallack—

> " How fearful
> And dizzy 'tis to cast one's eyes so low,
> The crows and choughs, that wing the midway air
> Show scarce so gross as beetles :————
> ———————————— I'll look no more,
> Lest my brain turn, and the deficient sight
> Topple down headlong."

This is undoubtedly one of the most extraordinary and surprising places in the mining districts of Cornwall, whether considered for the rare and rich assemblage of its minerals, or for the wild and stupendous character of its rock scenery. Surely, if ever a spot seemed to bid defiance to the successful efforts of the miner, it was the site of the *Crown Engine** at Botallack, where at the very commencement of his subterranean labours, he was required to lower a steam engine down a precipice of more than two hundred feet, with the view of extending his operations under the bed of the Atlantic ocean!!! There is something in the very idea which alarms the imagination; and the situation and appearance of the gigantic machine, together with the harsh jarring of its bolts, re-echoed from the surrounding rocks, are well calculated to excite our astonishment.

But if you are thus struck and surprised at the scene when viewed from the cliff above, how much greater will be your wonder if you descend

---

* " *Crown Engine,*" so named from its vicinity to three rocks called the " *Three Crowns.*"

It was our intention to have presented the reader with an engraving of this extraordinary scene, and indeed measures had been taken for its accomplishment, when we were induced to abandon the design on learning that a lithographic print had been published by a meritorious and self-taught artist at Penzance, the sale of which we were anxious not to diminish.

to the surface of the mine. You will then behold a combination of the powers of art with the wild sublimity of Nature which is quite unparalleled; the effects of the whole being not a little heightened by the hollow roar of the raging billows which are perpetually lashing the cliff beneath. In looking up you will observe troops of mules laden with sacks of coals, for the supply of the engine, with their undaunted riders, fearlessly trotting down the winding path which you trembled at descending even on foot. As you approach the engine, the cliff becomes almost perpendicular, and the ore raised from the mine is therefore drawn up over an inclined plane,* by means of a horse engine placed on the extreme verge of the overhanging rocks above, and which seems to the spectator below as if suspended in *" mid air."*

The workings of this mine extend at least seventy fathoms in length under the bed of the sea; and in these caverns of darkness are many human beings, for a small pittance, and even that of a precarious amount, constantly digging for ore, regardless of the horrors which surround them, and of the roar of the Atlantic ocean, whose boisterous waves are incessantly rolling over their

---

* This apparatus is termed " *The Shammel Whim.*"

heads. We should feel pity for the wretch who, as an atonement for his crimes, should be compelled to undergo the task which the Cornish miner voluntarily undertakes, and as cheerfully performs; yet such is the force of habit, that very rarely does any other employment tempt him to forsake his own; the perils of his occupation are scarcely noticed, or if noticed, are soon forgotten.

The *Lode** of the mine may be seen *cropping out*, in the group of rocks beneath the engine. The ore is the grey and yellow sulphuret of copper, mixed with the oxide of tin,† of which *she‡* has already "*turned up*" a sufficient quantity to afford a very handsome premium to the adventurers. In the grey sulphuret of this mine, *purple copper ore*, of the kind called by the Germans "*Buntkupfererz*," is frequently met with. Besides which, a great number of interesting minerals may be collected, as several varieties of *Jasper*; *arborescent native Copper*; *Jaspery iron ore*; *Arseniate of Iron*, which until it was discovered in the *Crown lode* of Botallack, was un-

---

* A metalliferous vein is provincially called a *Lode*.

† The tin and copper are in a state of *mechanical* mixture, although *Dr. Boase* has lately found amongst the heaps, a specimen of "*Tin Pyrites*," in which these metals are *chemically* combined.

‡ The miners always distinguish their mines by a *feminine* appellation.

known in St. Just. It is of a brown colour, and is crystallized in cubes. *Sulphuret of Bismuth,* imbedded in *Jasper*; beautiful *specular iron ore ; hœmatitic Iron*; and the *hydrous oxide of iron,* in prisms terminated by pyramids, and which was supposed by the Count de Bournon to contain *Titanium.* The picturesque rocks of this district may be considered as composed of *Hornblende rock,* which will be found to alternate with slate. The contorted appearance of the former in the vicinity of Botallack is very singular, and will admit of much speculation. The *Crown rocks,* to which the mineralogist must not neglect to descend, consist of extremely compact *Hornblende rock,* in which occur numerous veins and beds of different minerals; viz. *veins of Garnet rock,* with numerous imbedded crystals, being at one part almost a foot in width; *Magnetic Iron Pyrites,* massive, in beds, near the engine; its colour is bluish-grey, and it is called by the workmen *Spelter,* who mistake it probably for *Blende,* which latter mineral also occurs here in considerable quantities. In a part of the rock, which is almost inaccessible, there is a vein of *Epidote,* distinctly crystallized, and about six inches wide. The miners, however descend the fearful precipice without any difficulty, in order to collect specimens for the inquisitive visitant. *Axinite* also occurs in veins, or perhaps in beds ; *Thallite, Chlorite, Tremolite,* and a black crystallized *Schorl,* in which the late Rev. William Gregor detected six per cent. of *Titanium,* are to be found also in this interesting spot.

CAPE CORNWALL is the next object of interest after Botallack. This point of land stretches out to the west, at an elevation of two hundred and thirty feet, and forms the northern boundary of *Whitsand Bay* (p. 88). It is entirely composed of a slaty rock, traversed by numerous veins of *Actinolite.* To the geologist this spot will be interesting, since on the shore beneath, a junction may be observed between the *Granite* of the Land's End, and the slate of this promontory.* These formations are separated by a large vein of *metalliferous quartz,* which forms the *lode* of the mine in the neighbourhood, called " *Little Bounds,*" and whose engine suspended in the cliff above, constitutes a very striking feature in the scenery. This vein, besides *Oxide of Tin,* for which it is worked, contains *Native Copper,* different *Oxides of Iron, Red Jasper, Quartz* of a bright brownish red colour, and *Scaly red Iron*

---

* See a paper by Dr. John Davy, in the first volume of the Transactions of the Royal Geological Society of Cornwall, entitled ·· *On the Granite Veins of Porth Just.*"

ore, sometimes investing Quartz, and occasionally in small masses consisting of red cohering scales, which are unctuous to the touch.

Mr. Carne states, that in this mine three distinct lodes, distant from each other, have been worked under the sea; two of them being in granite, the third in slate. Here also, at two parts of the *lode,* known by the name of " *Save-all's lode,*" probably, as the name would seem to imply, in consequence of the avarice of the miner, a communication has been made between the sea and the mine; one of them is at about high water mark at spring tides; the other is covered by the sea at every tide, except at very low neaps; great and constant attention is therefore necessary for the security of this latter breach. At first the opening was stopped by a piece of wood covered with turf; but as this defence was not found to be sufficiently secure, a thick platform caulked like the deck of a ship, was ultimately placed upon it, and which renders it nearly water proof. The breaking of the waves is heard in all the levels of the mine, and in the part directly beneath the pebbly beach, the rolling of the stones in boisterous weather produces a most terrific effect. In the drift at the forty fathom level, which is carried a considerable way under the

sea, Mr. Chenhalls, the intelligent agent of the
mine, had formerly observed a successive formation of *Stalactites*; in consequence of which statement, Dr. John Davy and Mr. Majendie were
induced to visit the spot. It had been closed for
two years previously, but before it was shut up
Mr. Chenhalls had carefully removed all the
Stalacites which then existed. Upon examination
it was observed that a fresh crop had been produced during the interval just stated; some of
which were eighteen inches in length, and above
an inch in diameter. The *Stalagmites* directly
underneath them were of still larger dimensions;
both however had the same yellowish-brown colour, and were found to consist of *Peroxide of
iron.* Specimens may be seen in the cabinet at
Penzance. Dr. Paris has suggested that they
resulted from the decomposition of *Pyrites*, forming, in the first instance, a soluble *Sulphate* of
iron, but which, by attracting farther oxygen,
deposited its base in the form here discovered.

At a little distance southward of Cape Cornwall, is a high rocky promontory called CARA-
GLOSE HEAD, from which the traveller may
command one of the most interesting views in
this part of Cornwall. On the north are Cape
Cornwall, and the romantic machinery of *Little*

Bounds Mine. Southward and directly under the head, the interesting creek called PORNANVON COVE, with the engine of *Huel St. Just Tin Mine* near the sea shore. Westward, on a clear day, the Scilly Islands may be distinctly seen. This is a spot seldom visited by strangers, but with the exception of Botallack, it is certainly one of the most striking in the district of Saint Just. At *Pornanvon Cove*, a stratum of sea sand and pebbles may be seen in the cliff, at an elevation of fifteen feet above high water mark !

Advancing from the coast into the interior of the country towards Saint Just's *Church-town,* Dr. Berger observed many blocks of *Schorl rock** scattered on this part of the granitic plain, particularly amongst the rubbish of some old tin mines, which are here very numerous, but are now quite deserted.

SAINT JUST CHURCH TOWN. Nothing of any interest is to be seen at this place, except a very

---

*·This rock is a binary compound of *Quartz* and *Schorl,* without any, or scarcely any, admixture of the other constituents of Granite; and yet when we consider its various relations, it must be regarded as rather a variety of the latter than a distinct rock. The locality now mentioned and that singular group of rocks between Truro and Bodmin, known by the name of *Roach Rock*, are, as far as we know, the only places in Cornwall where this modification of granite is found *in mass.* In the form of veins its occurrence is not unusual, especially at the junction of granite and slate, where it would often seem to exist as an intermediate rock.

ancient cross, a sketch of which we shall introduce at the conclusion of the present chapter;
and the remains of an ancient Amphitheatre.

In this, and similar " *Rounds,*" as they are
provincially called, the ancient British assembled,
in order to witness those athletic sports, for which
the Cornish are still remarkable; indeed, at this
very day, Wrestling matches are held in the amphitheatre at Saint Just, during the holidays of
Easter and Whitsuntide.

The Antiquary ought not to quit this parish
without visiting the " *Botallack Circles*;" when
examined separately they do not differ essentially
from that at *Bolleit,* or at *Boscawen Un* before
described (p. 81); but they intersect each other
and form a confused cluster; " but in this seem-

+ The Cornish have ever been celebrated for their skill in the art
of Wrestling; hence the expression " *To give one a Cornish Hug,*"
which is a dexterous lock in that art peculiar to them. It must,
however, be admitted, whether as a matter of triumph or humilia-
tion, we will not declare, that the Cornish have greatly declined
in their art, so as to be now inferior even to the Devonians, and to
the inhabitants of many other districts in their prowess. This degeneracy might perhaps be attributed to the change which has
taken place during the lapse of time, in the mode of working for
Tin; formerly it was all procured by *Streaming,* an occupation as
healthy and invigorating, as the present one of subterranean mining
is debilitating. We apprehend, however, that a moral cause of
still greater force has contributed to the change—the diffusion of
Methodism; which has unquestionably proved a powerful instrument in the amelioration of the habits and disposition of the Cornish
miner.

ing confusion," exclaims Dr. Borlase, " I cannot
but think that there was some mystical meaning,
or, at least, distinct allotment to particular uses ;
some of these might be employed for the sacrifice;
others allotted to prayer, others to the feasting
of the priests, others for the station of those who
devoted the victims; and lastly, that these circles intersected each other in so remarkable a
manner, as we find them in this monument, might
be to intimate that each of these holy rites, though
exercised in different circles, were but so many
links of one and the same chain, and that there
was a constant dependance and connection between sacrifice, prayer, holy feasting, and all the
several parts of Druidical worship."

In taking leave of the metalliferous district of
Saint Just we have to observe, that it has been
considered by Mr. Carne, and not without probability, as having constituted the principal portion of what was formerly known under the name
of the *Cassiterides*, and that if it would redound
to the honour, or contribute to the prosperity of
Saint Just, it might be said, " that her Tin was
probably a constituent part of the Shield and
Helmet of Achilles,—of the Tabernacle of the
Israelites,—of the Purple of Tyre,—and of the
Temple of Solomon."

From Saint Just's *Church-town*, the road con-
ducts us over a wild part of the peninsula, although highly salubrious, and invigorating from
the fine sea breezes which blow from every side;
after a ride over such bleak and barren hills, the
eye experiences a singular repose on our approach to the cultivated shores of the Mount's
Bay.

Saint Just.

EXCURSION IV.

TO SAINT IVES, HAYLE, HUEL ALFRED, &c.

PASSING through the little village of Chyandour, we ascend by a shady road through that of
Gulval, to *Kenegie,** the seat of the family of
John Arundel Harris Arundel, Esq. This spot
commands a very interesting view of the Mount's
Bay, the beauty of which is greatly heightened
by the diversified and picturesque foreground.
On a neighbouring hill is *Rosmorran,* the retired cottage ornée of George John, Esq. of Penzance; we scarcely know a situation where the
skill of the landscape gardener could be exerted
with greater advantage or effect.

Pursuing the road, and passing the gate of
Kenegie, we ascend the great granite range
which extends from Dartmoor to the Land's
End, and which appears, in this part of the

---

* Kenegie became the seat of the younger branch of Harris of
Heyne, in about the year 1600.

country, to be broken into a number of detached groups. Upon the summit of one of these hills stands a castellated building which, although of modern construction, occupies the site of an ancient " hill castle, called " *Castle an Dinas* ;" it was erected by John Rogers, Esq., as a picturesque object from his occasional residence at *Treassowe.*

On descending the northern side of the granite ridge, a curious atmospheric phenomenon is frequently observable,—the clear and cloudless sky becoming suddenly dense and hazy ; the change is evidently occasioned by the condensation of the vapours contained in the warm and rarefied air of the Mount's Bay, by the colder one which blows from the Bristol channel. Amidst wild and rugged hills the road winds to Saint Ives, in the course of which, the geologist will have many opportunities of furnishing his portfolio with sketches, in illustration of the changes which time and weather produce on Granite; hugh blocks of this stone lie scattered on all sides, while stupendous masses are seen on the hills above in different stages of decomposition, and which from their threatening attitude, would appear as if in preparation to join their former companions in the plains below.

SAINT IVES. This populous sea port and borough stands on the shores of the Bristol Channel, in a very fine bay bounded by bold rocks of *Greenstone* and *Slate.* The latter of these rocks is in many places undergoing rapid decomposition, in consequence of which large masses of the Hornblende rock have fallen in various directions, and given a singular character of picturesque rudeness to the scene : this is remarkably striking in the group of rocks which constitute Godrevy Island.

Saint Ives is a populous sea port, of very considerable antiquity, deriving its name from that of *Iia,* a religious woman, who came hither from Ireland in about the year 460. The Corporation, which obtained its powers from a charter granted by Charles the First, consists of a mayor, recorder, town-clerk, twelve capital burgesses, and twenty-four inferior burgesses. The Borough returns two members to Parliament, a privilege which was conferred in the fifth year of Queen Mary; and the right of election was vested in all the householders in the parish paying scot and lot. In the year 1816, the magistrates, and trustees of the Pier and Port of Saint Ives resolved to extend the former, and to construct a breakwater, in order to shelter it. The under-

K

taking has been commenced, but it is at present far from being completed.

Saint Ives is the birth place of the *Reverend Jonathan Toup*, Rector of Saint Martin's near Looe, the learned annotator of *Suidas*, and editor of *Longinus*. His father was formerly the lecturer of this town.

On no part of the Cornish coast is the Pilchard fishery carried on with greater activity or success; and at the time of large draughts, it is usual for all the inhabitants to contribute their assistance; shops and dwelling-houses are frequently deserted on such occasions, and even the church has been abandoned, when large shoals have made their appearance on the Sabbath! By a certain signal given by a person stationed on the heights, the approach of a shoal is generally announced to the town; the effect is most singular. Trumpets are immediately heard in different parts, and the inhabitants rushing from their houses, and quitting their ordinary occupations, are to be seen running in all directions, and vociferating the word " *Hever—Hever— Hever.*"—What the term signifies, or whence it was derived, no one can conjecture, but its sound is no less animating to the ears of a Saint Ivesman, than is the cry of " *To Arms,*" to the Son of Mars; and the tumult which it excites is more like that of a besieged city, than the peaceable and joyful bustle of an industrious fishing town.

As we have not hitherto described the manner in which the Pilchard Fishery is conducted, perhaps the present will be an appropriate opportunity.

The Pilchard, in size and form, very much resembles the common Herring,* and is actually confounded with it by Linnæus, under the name of " *Clupœa Harengus*;" upon close inspection, however, an essential difference may be readily discovered. The Pilchard is less compressed, as well as smaller; there is besides a very simple, and common test of distinction, depending upon the dorsal fin of the Pilchard being placed exactly in the centre of gravity, if therefore it be taken up by this fin, it will preserve an equilibrium; while the body of the Herring, when so tried, will dip towards the head. Mr. Pennant likewise observes that the scales of the latter easily drop off, whereas those of the Pilchard adhere very closely.

It has been commonly stated that these fish

---

* There is also a very considerable similarity in their mode of migration. The word *Herring* is derived from the German " *Heer*," an Army, to express their numbers, and order of array.

migrate from the North sea in immense shoals, during the summer months, and reach the Cornish coast about the middle of July, where they remain until the latter end of September, when they again depart to the arctic regions. This statement, however, cannot be correct, as the fish are never seen off the coasts of Scotland, the northern shores of Ireland, the Isle of Man, nor, in fact, off any coast north of Cornwall. It would therefore seem more probable, that they come from some part of the Western ocean, and return thither at the end of the season. Within the last ten years a considerable alteration in their usual course has taken place, much to the disappointment of the Cornish Fishermen; they have kept at a greater distance from the shores; whether this circumstance has arisen from their food being farther than usual out at sea, or from any alteration in the currents, it is impossible to ascertain. In the present year, however, they seem to have returned to Saint Ives; an immense quantity, calculated at three thousand hogsheads, having been taken at one " *catch,*" by two *Seines* in this bay. The other parts of the coast have been visited only by very small shoals.

The preparations for this fishery are generally

commenced about the end of July,* as the period at which the Pilchards are expected to pay their annual visit. As they usually make their appearance here in the evening, the boats engaged in the adventure seldom go to sea before three or four o'clock in the afternoon, and as rarely remain longer than ten. On some occasions, however, they go out again very early in the morning, and have sometimes succeeded in taking fish at sun rise. The fishermen, arranged in boats which are scattered at a little distance from each other, are directed to the shoals by persons who are stationed on the cliffs, or who sometimes follow in boats. These persons who are called " *Huers*," probably from the *hue and cry* which they raise, discover them by the peculiar red tint† which the water assumes, and from other

---

* The first outfit of a Seine, with its boats, oars, ropes, sails, nets, and a quantity of salt sufficient to cure five hundred hogsheads of fish, if purchased new, cannot be estimated at less than a Thousand pounds. The preparations for the water consists of three boats, i. e. two large ones and a small one; each large boat containing seven men, and in the small one are the master, another man, and two boys. The " *Seine Boat* " and the " *Follower*" are the names by which the two large boats are distinguished ; and the small one is called the " *Lurker*."

† The whiteness of the sand in the Bay of St. Ives renders the shoals of fish easily distinguishable, and contributes very greatly to the success of the fishery upon this coast.

indications with which they are well acquainted.*
The spot where the nets should be cast, or " *shot*"
having been determined from the signals of the
Huer," the boat containing the great net or " *Stop
Seine*" as it is called, and which is frequently as
much as 300 fathoms in length, and 10 in depth,
is gradually cast from the boat into the sea by
two men, as the vessel is gently rowed round the
shoal by others of the crew; a service which is
performed with such dexterity that in less than
four minutes the whole of this enormous net is
shot, and the fish enclosed. Upon this occasion
it is always the first care of the *Seiner* to secure
that part to which the fish were swimming; and
then so to carry the net around them, that they
shall be hemmed in on every side. The net immediately spreads itself, the corks on one edge
rendering it buoyant, and the leaden weights on
the other causing it to sink to the bottom; for if
the depth of the water should exceed that of the
Seine, it is evident that there would be little

---

* The *Tunny* fish in the Archipelago was caught by a similar
process, " Ascendebat quidam (Anglice the *Huer,* Græce *Thun-
noscopos*) in ultum promontorium, unde Thunnorum gregem spe-
cularetur, quo viso, signum piscatoribus dabat, qui ratibus totum
gregem includebant." *Vide Blomfield's Notes on the Persæ of
Eschylus, p.* 148. The seine was as familiar to the Athenians, as
the Pilchard fishery is to the inhabitants of Cornwall; and it is
said that Eschylus took great delight in witnessing it.

probability of securing any fish, however large
the shoal might be. As the circle in which the
Seine is shot, is generally larger than the net can
compass, its two extremities are at a distance
from each other when the whole is in the water.
Ropes are therefore carried out from each of
these ends, by which they are *warped* together
by the men on board the two large boats, so as to
bring them into contact. When this is effected,
the two extremities, if the shoal be large, are
lifted from the bottom, and expeditiously tacked
together. During this last operation every method is adopted to agitate the water, and drive
back the body of fish from this only aperture
through which they can escape. This having
been accomplished, the fish remain within the
enclosure formed by the encircling net, which
extends from the surface to the bottom of the
sea. It only now remains to secure the Seine in
its position, for which purpose *grapnels*, or small
anchors, are carried out at some distance on
every side, the ropes from which are fastened to
the rope at the upper end of the net; these *grapnels* will of course retain the Seine in its circular
position, and preserve it against the influence of
the tides, and the changes of the weather. Where,
however, the shore is sandy and shelving, as in

Saint Ives' Bay, the *Seine* is at once drawn into
shallow water by a number of men, who are
called " *Blowsers.*"

The quantity of fish which is thus secured will
depend of course on many contingent circumstances, such for instance, as the strength of the
tides, the nature of the coast, and the dexterity
of the fishermen, &c. A Seine has sometimes
enclosed as many as fifteen hundred, or two
thousand hogsheads. The next operation is to
remove the fish from the Seine, and to convey
them in boats to the shore. This is performed
by another smaller net, termed a " *Tuck net,*"
and the process is called " *Tucking,*" and is a
sight which the stranger should not, on any account, neglect to witness. This busy scene always takes place at low water, and when it happens on one of those calm evenings which so
frequently occur in the summer season, it is impossible to imagine a more exquisite scene. The
moon shedding her lustre on the sea displays its
surface covered with vessels, sailing or rowing
in all directions to the Seine, whilst her beams
by striking upon the dripping fish as they are
poured, by baskets, from the *tuck net* into boats,*

* The boats which attend for the purpose of conveying the fish
from the *tuck net* to the shore are termed " *Dippers,*" the proprie-

produce an appearance which resembles a stream of liquid silver.

There is another mode of catching Pilchards by " *Driving Nets,*" * which are drawn after their respective boats, fastened only at one end; in the meshes of which the fish are arrested as they attempt to pass. This species of fishery is always carried on at a considerable distance from the shore, lest, by approaching too near the land they should disperse the shoals which the *Seiner* is waiting to enclose. The quantity thus taken is very small; but the fish are remarkably fine, and the expense of the adventure is comparatively trifling.

The fish, having been brought to the fish cellars, undergo the process of being " *cured;*" which is performed by laying them up in broad piles, " *in bulk,*" as it is called, and salting them as they are piled up, with bay salt. In this situation they generally remain for forty days, although the time allowed for their lying *in bulk* is often

---

tors of which are differently compensated in different places; they either receive a certain proportion of the fish, as from one-fourth to one-sixth, according to the distance from the shore, or else they receive a certain sum of money for each boat load. When the fish are caught in the night, fires are instantly kindled on the nearest shore, as a signal for the boats in the bay to repair to the spot.

* These nets are of far greater antiquity than the *Seine,* the latter having been introduced from Ireland.

regulated by the interests of the merchant, who, it may be supposed, is ever ready to avail himself of any favourable turn in the foreign markets. The period directed by Government is that of thirty-three days. During this process a great quantity of oil, blood, and dirty pickle, drains from the fish; and which, from the inclination of the floor, immediately find their way into a receptacle placed for their reception.* The Pilchards, when taken from the bulk, are carried to large troughs, in which they are washed, and completely cleansed from the salt, filth, and coagulated oil which they had acquired.† They are then packed into hogsheads, and pressed by a strong lever, for the purpose of squeezing out the oil, which issues through a hole at the bottom of the cask; the pressing continues for a week, and formerly ten gallons of oil were procured from every hogshead, but at this time, not more than four can be obtained; such a change in the fatness of the fish is not easily to be explained. The hogsheads are now *headed up*, and exported to the different ports of the Mediterranean, princi-

---

* These dregs are sold to the curriers, at about sixteen pence per gallon.

† The skimmings which float on the water in which the pilchards are washed, bear the name of *Garbage*, and are sold to the soap-boilers.

pally to' the Italian ports; and upon every hogshead so exported, Government allows a bounty
of 8s 6d.   Upwards of 30,000 hogsheads are annually consumed in England; 'and above 100,000
have been exported in one year.   The quantity
of salt necessary to cure a hogshead of fish is estimated at about 300 lbs. and the expense of the
whole for that quantity, including the cask, salt,
labour, &c. is from £1 : 3s to £1 : 6s ; and it has
been calculated that the bounty, together with
the value of the oil (from £20 to £28 per ton),
will in general reimburse the whole expense.

This fishery is in every respect of the highest
importance to the county of Cornwall, affording
employment to at least twelve thousand persons,*
whilst the capital engaged cannot be fairly estimated at less than three hundred and fifty, or
four hundred thousand pounds.

The broken and refuse fish are sold at about
10d per bushel, for manure, and are used throughout the county with excellent effects, especially

---

* In salting, packing, pressing, and preparing the fish for the
market, there are at least 5000, 4-5ths of which are women ; the
rope-makers, blacksmiths, shipwrights, &c. upwards of 400 ; the
twine spinners are women, about 150 in number ; the makers
and menders of nets are chiefly women and children, in all about
600.   Nets are also made during the winter season, by the fishermen and their families.   These numbers are of course exclusive of
the seamen employed.

for raising all green crops; they are usually mixed with sand, or soil, and sometimes with sea weed, to prevent them from raising too luxuriant a crop, arising from a too rapid decomposition; thus employed their effects are very permanent, and there is a popular belief that a single pilchard will fertilize a foot square of land for several years; and certain it is, that after the apparent exhaustion of this manure, its powers may be again excited by ploughing in a small proportion of *quick lime*, which will produce a still further decomposition of the animal matter, and develope a fresh succession of those elements which are essential to the growth of vegetable substances.

The Herring fishery is also carried on to a great extent at Saint Ives; this fish appears after the pilchard has quitted the shores, and is much smaller than that which is caught on the northern coasts of Britain; which corroborates the general opinion, that the farther it migrates to the south, the more it decreases in size. It is also worthy of remark that, notwithstanding the great abundance of this fish in the Bristol Channel, it very seldom passes the Land's End, and is consequently rarely caught in the Mount's Bay, or on the southern shores of Cornwall.

But let us return from this digression, and proceed with our excursion.—

Quitting Saint Ives by the eastern road, we
are conducted along an elevated cliff, which
affords a complete command of every object in
the bay; in our route we pass *Tregenna Castle*,
the seat of Samuel Stephens, Esq. and on the
summit of a lofty hill, about a mile from this
mansion, stands a pyramid, which immediately
attracts the notice of the traveller, as well on
account of the singular wildness of its situation,
as the complete absence of every shrub, or rural
ornament, with which such objects are usually
associated. It was erected by the late eccentric
John Knill, Esq., a bencher of Gray's Inn, and
some time collector of the Port of Saint Ives, it
having been intended as a Mausoleum for the reception of his remains, although he afterwards
revoked this intention, and ordered his body to
be given to an anatomist in London, for dissec-
tion. On one side of this pyramid is inscribed,
" *Johannes Knill*," on another, " *Resurgam*,"
and on a third, " *I know that my Redeemer
liveth*." He directed in his will, that at the end
of every five years, a Matron and ten girls,
dressed in white, should walk in procession, with
music, from the market house at Saint Ives, to

this pyramid, around which they should dance, singing the hundredth Psalm!

———— " Pueri circum innuptæque puellæ
Sacra canunt."

For the purpose of keeping up this custom, he bequeathed some freehold lands, which are vested in the officiating minister, the mayor, and the collector of the port of Saint Ives, who are allowed Ten Pounds for a dinner. The first celebration of these *Quinquennial rites* excited, as may easily be supposed, very considerable interest throughout the western parts of the county.

" No tongue was mute, nor foot was still,
But *One and All** were on the hill,
In chorus round the tomb of Knill."

The report which was drawn up at the time by an eye witness of these festivities, exhibits such an admirable specimen of the *mock Heroic*, that we feel assured that the tourist will thank us for having given insertion to it in the Appendix.

Pursuing the road along the cliff we pass *Lelant* church, and arrive at the river *Hayle*, which takes its rise near Crowan, and falls into Saint Ives Bay; although it arrives at the level of the sea three miles before it reaches the northern coast, and winds its way through an area of sand,

---

* *One and All*,—the motto of the Cornish arms.

nearly half a mile wide, and more than two miles
long; this sand, at high water, is generally sub-
merged, so that the traveller who wishes to cross
is. obliged to take a circuitous route over the
bridge at *Saint Erth*; but upon the ebbing of
the tide, it soon becomes fordable, and may be
passed over even by foot passengers. It is a
curious circumstance that at twelve o'clock at
noon, and at midnight, it is *always* fordable;
this apparent paradox is solved by knowing, that
at *Spring tides* it is always low water at these
hours, and that the *Neap tides* never rise sufficiently high to impede the passage.

The Port of Hayle is situated on the eastern
side of the river, where a great trade is carried
on with Wales for timber, coals,* iron, and limestone; and with Bristol, for earthen-ware, gro-
ceries, &c. It is also one of the principal places
of export for the copper ore of the western mines.
In the former edition of this work we described
the processes by which the *smelting* and *refining*
of Copper were conducted at this place, but as it
was acknowledged to be much cheaper to carry
the ore to the coal, than to bring the coal to the
ore, the proprieters found themselves compelled

---

* Cornwall is exempted from the payment of any duties on coal,
so far as it is used for the working of the mines.

to abandon the speculation. The buildings in the neighbourhood, however, still continue as memorials of the former existence of such works, having been constructed with square masses of the *scoria*,* which had been cast into moulds for such purposes, as it issued from the furnace. In the museum of the Geological Society at Penzance the stranger may see an interesting model of this *Copper House,* and of the furnaces employed in the reduction of the ore.

There are now at Hayle two very extensive Iron Founderies, in which are cast the largest engines which have been hitherto erected on mines. They are wrought partly by water, and partly by Steam Engines. Near the Copper House the traveller will not fail to notice the fine back-water dam, which was constructed about thirty years since, for the scouring out of the harbour. The effect has been a considerable reduction of the sand which forms its bottom, so that ships of much greater burden may now enter it. The plan and execution of this work, which was undertaken at the expense of the then exist-

---

* All the walls in the neighbourhood are built of the same material ; and since these vitreous cubes are so piled upon each other as to leave interstices, it has been facetiously observed that " *in Cornwall the walls are built of glass, and that you may distinctly see through them.*"

ing Hayle Copper Company, reflect great credit on the late *John Edwards, Esq.*, who first conceived its practicability and advantage, and under whose direction it was completed. A phenomenon occurred at these works some years ago which afforded a curious illustration of the secret and destroying agency of Galvanic electricity. The flood gates were found to undergo a very rapid decay, which was perfectly inexplicable, until the engineer ascertained that it depended entirely upon the contact of iron and copper bolts and braces, which had been introduced into the different parts of the frame work.

The country around Hayle is entirely desolated with sand, consisting of minutely comminuted marine shells, and which, with some few interruptions extends all along the coast, from Saint Ives to near Padstow, and in many places is drifted into hills of sixty feet in elevation. There can be but little doubt that this sand was originally brought from the sea side by hurricanes, but not even a popular tradition remains of the time or manner of this extensive devastation, which has reached, with some distinct intervals, nearly forty miles in length. Some allusion to this event has been supposed to have been discovered amongst the ancient records of the Arundel family, fixing

L

the period about the twelfth century; but *Mr. Boase* observes, that the fact of the churches still remaining more or less ingulphed, the age of which does not much exceed three centuries, decisively refutes such a conjecture. On the other hand, it would appear that in the *liber valorum* of Henry the Eighth, the living of *Gwythian* was estimated far above its proportion to adjoining parishes. By the shifting of the sand by high winds, the tops of houses, and the ruins of ancient buildings, may be occasionally seen at this very day; and in some places a great number of human bones have been discovered, derived from the cemetries which have been formerly inundated.

The farther progress of the sand flood is at length arrested by extensive plantations of the *Arundo Arenaria*, or common sea rush.*

The most important geological circumstance connected with the history of this sand is, that

---

* The value of this useful rush in checking the progress of sand, has been long known; there was an act of parliament in Scotland, so long ago as the year 1695, to prevent persons who collected this rush (then known by the name of *Starre* or *Bent*) for the purpose of making mats, from plucking it up, and thereby loosening the sand. A clause to the same effect was introduced into a multifarious act of parliament in the year 1742. The operation of this clause extends generally to the north-west coast of England; but such persons as claimed prescriptive right of cutting it on the sea coast of Cumberland are exempted from its operation.

on several parts of the coast, it is passing into the state of a solid compact rock! The fact was first investigated by Dr. Paris, who has published a memoir upon the subject in the first volume of the Transactions of the Geological Society of Cornwall; and as every scientific traveller must be desirous of exploring so interesting a pheno- menon we have extracted, from the paper above mentioned, such notices as may be useful in assisting his researches.

" The *Sandstone* which occurs on the northern coast of Cornwall undoubtedly affords one of the most splendid and instructive instances of a *Recent Formation* upon record. We actually detect Nature at work in changing calcareous sand into stone; and she does not refuse admit- tance into her manufactory, nor does she conceal with her accustomed reserve the details of the operations in which she is engaged. It does not however appear that any geologist has fully availed himself of so rare an indulgence;—to drop the allegory, no complete or satisfactory explanation has been hitherto afforded of this most interesting formation, nor of the phenomena which attend it. At the period that Dr. Borlase wrote his History of Cornwall, the science of Chemistry had scarcely dawned; we cannot therefore feel surprised at his having attributed ' *the concretion of shelly sand to the agglutinating quality of sea water.*"

" The sand first appears in a slight, but encreasing state of aggregation on several parts of the shore in the Bay of Saint Ives; but on approaching the Gwythian river it becomes more extensively indurated. On the shore opposite to Godrevy Island, an immense mass occurs of more than a hundred feet in depth, containing entire shells and fragments of clay-slate; and it is singular that the whole mass should assume a very striking appearance of stratification. In some places, it appears that attempts have been made to separate it, probably for the purpose of building, for several old houses in Gwythian are entirely built with it. The rocks in the vicinity of this recent formation in the Bay of Saint Ives are *Greenstone* and *Clay-slate*, which appear to alternate. But it is around the promontory of *New Kaye*, in Fistrel Bay, in the parish of Saint Columb Minor, that the geologist will be most struck with this formation, for here there is scarcely any other rock in sight. The cliffs, which are high and extend for several miles, are wholly composed of it, and are occasionally intersected by veins and dykes of *Breccia.* In the cavities hang calcareous stalactites of rude appearance. The beach is covered with disjointed fragments, which have been detached from the cliff above, many of which weigh at least from two to three tons. The sandstone is also to be here seen in different stages of induration; from a state in which it is too friable to be detached from the rock upon which it reposes without crumbling, to a hardness so considerable as to require a very violent blow from a hammer to break it;* indeed holes are actually bored in some parts for the purpose of admitting cables with which vessels are moored. Buildings are here commonly constructed of it, and the church of Crantock is entirely built with it. By the inhabitants the stone is employed for various articles of domestic and rural œconomy."

" The Geologist, who has previously examined the celebrated specimen from Guadaloupe, enclosing a human skeleton, and which is now in the British Museum, will be forcibly struck with the great similitude which this stone bears to it; and suspecting that masses might be found containing human bones imbedded, if a diligent search were made in the vicinity of those ceme-

* A highly illustrative series of this rock is deposited in the Geological Cabinet at Penzance.

tries which have been overwhelmed, 1 made an excursion with my friend Sir ChristopherHawkins, for that purpose ; but time and patience failed us, and the discovery is reserved for some more persevering and fortunate member of the society."

" Such then is the nature and situation of this most interesting formation. In the next place, we have to enquire into the causes which have operated in thus consolidating the sand, and into the peculiar circumstances under which the operation has been conducted."

" It will appear that there are at least three distinct modes by which the *lapidification* of calcareous sand may be effected, and that the present formation is capable of affording characteristic examples of each."

" The three species of cementing matter to which I allude, are all deposited from water in which they either exist chemically dissolved, or mechanically suspended. The water deriving them from the substances through which it percolates ; thus is the first species of cement obtained—

1. *By the percolation of water, through a stratum of calcareous sand, by which it becomes impregnated with carbonate of lime.*

2. *By the percolation of water through strata containing decomposing Sulphurets ; by*

which it becomes impregnated with Sul-
phuric salts.

3. *By the percolation of water through decom-*
posing Clay-slate, or any other ferruginous
strata; by which it becomes impregnated
with Iron, Alumina, and other mineral
matter.

In the first case, the very small proportion of
carbonate of lime which is held in solution will
necessarily render it a powerful cement, since the
density and compactness of a precipitate will generally vary, inversely as the rapidity with which it
is deposited. This fact is familiarly illustrated by
the obstinate adhesion of calcareous incrustations
to the interior surfaces of water decanters. In
the second case, wherein a sulphuric salt would
appear to act the part of a cement, it may be observed, that the *sulphatization of pyrites in the*
presence of calcareous matter is a very general
source of gypsum. The granular gypsum from
the Falls of Niagara, which is described by Dr.
Kidd as being " as white as snow," owes its
origin to a natural process of this decomposition;
for I am informed by Dr. Maclure of Philadel-
phia, who has visited the spot, that it is formed
in consequence of the action of water upon decomposing slate, which contains numerous veins

of *carbonate of lime* and *sulphate of iron.* I have also in my possession a series of incrustations which were taken out of steam boilers in Cornwall, one of which presents an admirable instance of the formation of *sulphate of lime*, its surface being beautifully studded with its crystals; the water which supplied the boiler, and by the evaporation of which this substance was deposited, was derived from a mine in clay-slate intersected with veins of *Pyrites* and *carbonate of lime.*"

" With regard to the third species of cementing matter, viz. *Oxide of Iron*, it is scarcely necessary to state, that in the induration of mineral bodies Iron has been long known to act a very important part; the most superficial observer must have noticed the concretions which so frequently appear on the beach around a rusty nail, or any fragment of iron, while the mineralogist must be acquainted with the proofs which Mr. Kirwan has collected in support of the fact. Nor is the part which it performs in the disintegration of mineral bodies less obvious; by its agency we have seen a loose sand become a hard rock, but if we extend our inquiry we shall find that *Iron* by attracting a farther proportion of *oxygen* from air or moisture, soon crumbles into dust, and thus proves the immediate cause of the decom-

position of that very rock, of which it formerly
constituted the indurating ingredient. In this, as
in every other operation, Nature preserves her
uniformity, producing the most diversified and
opposite effects by the modified application of
the same principles."

For this long digression we feel conscious that
some apology is necessary; the extreme interest
as well as novelty of the phenomenon will at
once suggest a sufficient excuse to the geologist;
and to other observers it may at least be pleaded
in extenuation, that they have lost nothing by
the delay, for it has been in a district which offers
but few objects of amusement or instruction.

About a mile and a half south-east of Hayle is
Huel Alfred, which was some years ago one of
the richest and most profitable Copper mines in
the county. The adventurers gained a clear
profit of nearly £130,000 during the period in
which it was wrought. In the year 1816, from
various causes, this mine was stopped, but about
six months ago a company of London gentlemen
embarked in the concern, and commenced their
operations in a very spirited manner. Before
Midsummer 1824, they expect to set at work two
steam-engines with cylinders of the immense size
of 90 inches in diameter, and one of less dimen-

sions. This mine will undoubtedly prove attractive and interesting to the mineralogist, as, during the last period of working, several curious and rare minerals were discovered, as *Stalactitic, swimming,* and *cubic quartz ; carbonate,* and *phosphate of Lead ; stalactitic, botryoidal,* and *investing Calcedony,* &c. The lodes of this mine are so large that should the stranger intend to visit the interior of the earth, he cannot select a better opportunity.

About a mile east of *Huel Alfred* are situated the *Herland Mines,* which, after an interval of twenty years, have been lately set at work again. The adventurers in these mines are also principally London capitalists, who have erected two steam-engines of which the cylinders are 80 inches in diameter. The mineralogist will not fail to visit mines which were celebrated for the beautiful specimens of *Native Silver, Vitreous Silver ore,* and *black oxide of Silver,* found there during the last period of its working, an account of which, by the Rev. M. Hitchins, was published in the Philosophical Transactions for the year 1801.

There is a remarkable contrast between the lodes of *Huel Alfred* and those of *Herland.* The former being few, but very large; the latter, small but very numerous, and the ore peculiarly rich.

The stranger may now proceed to Redruth, between which place and Hayle, there is a regular line of rich Copper mines, but as we propose to examine this metalliferous district in a future excursion, we shall return by *Saint Erth* to Penzance.

The desolate and barren appearance of the country in the neighbourhood of Hayle Sands, is much relieved by the woodland scenery of *Trevethoe*, the seat of the family of *Praed*; the father of the present possessor first introduced the *Pineaster Fir*, as a nurse for the growth of forest trees, and the estate of Trevethoe, as well as many others in the county, affords a striking evidence of the expediency of the plan. To the same gentleman we are indebted for the introduction of the *Arundo arenaria*, above mentioned.

Arriving at the bridge of *Saint Erth*, the traveller will perceive that a considerable portion of the breadth of the peninsula is here penetrated by an arm of the sea, and that the land which succeeds it in a direction towards the south is so low, that a canal might easily be cut along the hills which terminate at Marazion, and a communication be thus opened between the English and Irish Channels; or that an iron rail-way for the conveyance of coals, sand, &c. might be constructed at a comparatively small expense.

At *Saint Erth*, were formerly situated the " *Rolling Mills*" for reducing blocks, or bars of Copper, into flat sheets, as described in the first edition of this " Guide;" since, however, the Copper-works at Hayle have been abandoned, these mills have been used for rolling and hammering iron.

In the neighbourhood of *Saint Erth* is *Tredrea,* the Cornish residence of Davies Gilbert, Esq. M. P.

On our return to Penzance an opportunity occurs of witnessing the operation of *smelting* Tin ore.* It consists in first heating the ore,

---

* Tin appears to have been formerly smelted by the Jews, who in the reign of King John monopolized the tin trade, by merely hollowing out a plot of ground, and fusing the oxide with wood, in an open fire. Many ancient remains of this operation have been discovered in different parts of Cornwall, in which portions of metallic tin embedded in a stratum of charred wood, or charcoal, have been found; and which have given rise to the fallacy respecting the discovery of this metal in a *native state.* In examining a fragment of this kind which was found under the surface of a low and boggy ground in the parish of Kea, the late eminent chemist, *Mr. William Gregor*, observed a *vein of saline matter running through the mass*, which he ascertained to be *muriate of tin*; a full account of this interesting phenomenon is published in the first volume of the Transactions of the Cornish Society.

with about an eighth part of *Culm*,* in a rever-
batory furnace for six hours, during which period
the sulphur and arsenic are volatilized, and the
ore is reduced to its metallic state; the furnace
is then *tapped*, and the liquid metal *run out*; a
second melting, however, is necessary before it is
sufficiently pure to be cast into *blocks*,† and assayed at the Coinage. After this last melting,
and before the Tin is poured into the moulds, a
piece of green apple-tree wood is thrown into
the liquid metal, and kept under its surface; the
effect of which is to throw up the *scoria* with rapidity; it would seem to act merely in producing
a violent ebullition by the sudden disengagement
of steam. One hundred parts of the oxide of Tin
("Black Tin") at an average will yield about
65 parts of metal, or *White Tin*, as it is technically
termed.

Ludgvan Church, which appears upon an elevation on the right of the road leading to Penzance,
and which forms so prominent a feature on the
shores of the bay, will be visited by the Antiquary

---

* *Culm.* A species of very pure coal containing no sulphur.
It is imported from Wales.

† It is a favourite custom to dress a beef-steak on the pure Tin
in the mould, as soon as the surface becomes sufficiently hard to
bear it; and it must be admitted to be very far superior to that
which is cooked in the ordinary manner.

with sensations of respect, when he learns that it contains the mortal remains of Dr. Borlase the venerable and learned author of the Natural History and Antiquities of Cornwall. From the latin Inscription on his tomb it appears that he was fifty-two years rector of this parish, and that he died August 31st 1772, in the 77th year of his age. Although Dr. Borlase spent the greater part of a long life in this retired district, his fame as a scholar had spread through all the literary circles of the age. If we require any other testimony of his talents than that which his own works will afford, we may receive it from no less an oracle than POPE, with whom he regularly corresponded. In a letter written by the Poet, to express his thanks for the present of a Cornish diamond, presented by Dr. Borlase for the decoration of his grotto, Pope thus expresses himself, " I have received your gift, and have so placed it in my grotto, that it will resemble the donor— *in the shade, but shining.*"

If in the course of the present work we have ventured any remarks upon the opinions of Dr. Borlase which may be considered in the slightest degree disrespectful to his talents, we willingly offer this expiation at his shrine. His errors, whatever they may have been, were the inevitable consequence of the infant state of those sciences indirectly connected with his pursuits, not the result of literary incapacity, or of depraved judgment.

> " Custodiat Urnam
> Cana Fides, vigilentque perenni lampade Musæ."

About half a mile below the *Church-Town,* crossing the road to Marazion, is a *vallum* thrown up in the civil war by the Parliament forces when they besieged Saint Michael's Mount.

EXCURSION V.

TO REDRUTH, AND THE MINING DISTRICTS IN ITS
VICINITY.

——

In the present excursion, the traveller in search
of the Picturesque will meet with but meagre
fare ; for many a mile has the face of nature been
robbed of all ornament, and the interior of the
earth has been scattered over its surface in the
anxious pursuit of mineral treasures. The un-
sightly mounds of rubbish thus produced have
been accumulating for centuries, and are so highly impregnated with mineral matter that not a
blade of grass will vegetate upon them.

The intelligent traveller, however, must not
anticipate an excursion as destitute of interest
and variety as the surface of the country which
he is about to traverse, for like the shabby mien
of the miser, its aspect but ill accords with its
hoards; and the total absence of cultivation and
rural ornament, is soon forgotten amidst the

richest field of mineralogical enquiry which any country ever afforded.

As our present object is to afford the stranger such directions as may enable him to inspect this mining district with advantage, and to visit whatever is interesting and instructive in connection with it, it may in the first instance be expedient to offer a general outline of the modes in which the Cornish mines are worked, before we enter into the details of topographical description.

For many centuries* the Tin Mines in Cornwall have given to the country a very important place in the œconomical history of nations, and furnished a perpetual source of employment to a very large population, which exclusive of the artisans, tradesmen, and merchants, cannot be estimated at less than sixty thousand persons.

All the transactions connected with the Tin Mines are under the controul of the Stannary Laws. Courts are held every month, and they

---

* The Phœnicians traded upon the western coasts of Cornwall, for at least six hundred years before the birth of our Saviour, and that for the sake of Tin ;—so that the antiquity of our tin trade has been established upon mercantile principles for not less than twenty-four centuries. But in the earlier ages this metal was all procured from *Stream Works*, the method of working mines not having been known and practised for more than seven hundred years.

M

decide by juries of six persons, with a progressive appeal to the Lord Warden, and Lords of
the Duke of Cornwall's council; no custom,
however, or ancient law, prevails as to the working of Copper or Lead in the Stannaries, and
therefore all agreements are made upon such
terms as are decided on by the contracting
parties.

At present the greatest metallic product of the
county is Copper,* although this metal is, comparatively of modern discovery, and has not
been worked longer than a century. The reason
assigned for its having so long remained concealed is the assumed fact, that Copper generally
occurs at a much greater depth than Tin, and
that, consequently, the ancients for want of
proper machinery to drain off the water were
compelled to relinquish the metallic vein before
they reached the Copper; it is stated by Pryce,
in his *Mineralogia Cornubiensis,* as a general
rule, that Tin seldom continued rich and worth
working lower than 50 fathoms; but of late years
the richest Tin mines in Cornwall have been

---

* In the year 1822, the produce of the Copper mines in Cornwall amounted to 106,723 tons of ore, which produced 9,331 tons
in Copper, and £676,285 in money. Whereas the quantity of Tin
Ore raised did not exceed 20,000 tons.

much deeper. *Trevenen Mine* was 150,—*Hewas Downs* 140,—*Poldice* 120, and *Huel Vor* is now upwards of 130 fathoms in depth.

Upon the first discovery of Copper ore, the miner to whom its nature was entirely unknown, gave it the name of *Poder;* and it will hardly be credited in these times, when it is stated, that he regarded it not only as useless, but upon its appearance was actually induced to abandon the mine, the common expression upon such an occasion was, that " *the ore came in and spoilt the Tin.** About the year 1735, Mr. Coster, a mineralogist of Bristol, observed this said *Poder* among the heaps of rubbish, and seeing that the miners were wholly unacquainted with its value, he formed the design of converting it to his own advantage; he accordingly entered into a contract to purchase as much of it as could be supplied. The scheme succeeded, and Coster long continued to profit by Cornish ignorance.

The mines in the county of Cornwall consist chiefly of Tin and Copper, besides which there

---

* The Saxon Miners formerly regarded *Cobalt* in the same way. They considered it so troublesome when they found it among other ores, that a prayer was used in the German Church, *that God would preserve Miners from Cobalt, and from Spirits.*

are some which yield Lead*, Cobalt,† and Silver.‡ The ores are in veins which are provincially termed *Lodes*, the most important of which run in an east and west direction ; during their course they vary considerably in width, from that of a barley-corn to 36 feet ; ‖ the average may be stated at from one to four feet. It is, however, by no means regular, the same lode will vary in size from six inches to two feet, in the space of a few fathoms. No instance has yet occurred of lodes having been cut out in depth ; the deepest mine now at work is *Dolcoath*, which

---

* *Lead* is principally found in cross courses, or north and south veins. *Pentire Glaze*, near Padstow, which has lately produced the finest cabinet specimens of *Carbonate of Lead*, ever found in this country ; and *Huel Golding* in Perranzabuloe, are the principal mines in which the Lead occurs in cross courses. Lately, however, East and West Lodes of Lead have been discovered in the Parish of Newlyn, by Sir C. Hawkins, in draining a marsh. They are about two feet wide. Besides the Lead and a little quartz, they consist entirely of Clay ; neither Copper nor Tin have been seen in them. The Lead yields about Sixty Ounces of Silver per Ton.

† *Cobalt.* Huel *Sparnon* Tin and Copper Mine in the Parish of Redruth, is the only mine in the county that ever produced any considerable quantity of Cobalt ; one fragment raised from it weighed 1333 lbs.

‡ *Silver.* In the Copper Lode of Huel Ann, there occurred a distinct vein of *black* and *grey Silver ore,* with *Native Silver,* from two to five inches wide with a wall of Quartz, on each side. It was however very short. See Mr. Carne's paper on the Silver Mines of Cornwall, *Transactions of the Royal Geological Society of Cornwall, vol.* i. *p.* 118.

‖ Only one Lode in Cornwall has, however, been found of this size, and that only for the length of 20 fathoms in *Relistian*. In *Nangiles* the lode is, in some parts, 30 feet wide.

is about 235 fathoms from the surface to the lowest part.* *Crenver* and *Oatfield* have lately been stopped; they were 240 fathoms deep. The rocks through which the lodes descend are of different kinds, thus are Copper and Tin found in *granite,* as well as in *slate.*† The Tin in these veins‡ generally occurs in the state of an *oxide;* the only Copper ore of any consequence is *Copper Pyrites,* or Sulphuret of Copper; the *arseniates, carbonates,* &c. being too small in quantity to be of any importance in a mining point of view. *Iron* and *Arsenical Pyrites* are also very common attendants, and are both confounded under the name of *Mundic.* Besides the metalliferous veins which run easterly and westerly, we have already stated that there are others, not generally containing ore, which maintain a direction from North to South, and on that account are called *cross courses,* and often prove to the miner a great source of trouble and vexation;

---

* As the Counting House of Dolcoath has been determined to be 360 feet above the level of the sea, the mine extends 1050 feet below it; which is probably deeper under the sea level than any mine in the globe.

† Clay Slate is provincially called *Killas;* and Porphyry is known by the name of *Elvan.*

‡ For a full account of this subject, the reader must consult Mr. Carne's laborious paper, " *On the Veins of Cornwall,*" in the 2nd Volume of the Transactions of the Royal Geological Society of Cornwall.

for they not only cut through the other veins,
but frequently alter their position, or *heave* them,
as it is termed; and it is a very curious fact that
most of the *Tin* and *Copper* lodes, thus *heaved*,
are shifted in such a manner, as to be generally
found by turning to the *right* hand; *left* handed
heaves being comparatively rare. In *Huel Peever*
this vexatious phenomenon occurred, and it was
not until after a search of forty years that the
lode was recovered.*   The discovery of metalliferous veins is effected by various methods, the
most usual one is by sinking pits to the solid
rock, and then driving a trench north and south,
so as to meet with every vein in the tract through
which it passes; the process is a very ancient
one, and is termed *Costeening*.†   The operation,
however, of opening a new mine from the surface, or from *Grass*,‡ as it is called, is not one

---

* We must refer the reader to a Paper, " On the Veins of Corn-.
wall," by *W. Phillips, Esq*, published in the 2nd vol. of the
Transactions of the London Geological Society; and also to a
Paper, " On the relative Age of Veins," by *Joseph Carne, Esq.* in
the 2nd vol. of the Cornish Transactions.

† We shall pass over, as being too absurd to require any
serious refutation, the former belief in the power of the *Virgula
Divinatoria* to discover Lodes.   A power less poetical but not less
fabulous then the story of the *Virga Fatalis* that conducted Æneas
to the Shades.

‡ *Grass* is the technical name for the surface on all occasions.

of frequent occurrence.* The reworking of mines which have been formerly abandoned, on account of the produce being insufficient to pay the costs, from the fall of the standard price of ore, is quite sufficient to absorb all the speculative spirit of the country.

But by whatever accident or method a lode may be discovered, the leave of the proprietor of the soil must be obtained before any operations can be commenced, except in such cases of Tin Mines as are anciently *embounded* according to the provisions of the Stannary Laws. The owner of the land is technically called the *Lord,* whose share (which is termed his *Dish*) is generally one-sixth, or one - eighth of the profits; the parties who engage to work the mine are called *Adventurers,* their shares depending upon their original contributions and agreements.

When it has been determined to work a mine, three material points are to be considered; viz. the discharge of the water,—the removal of the barren rock and rubbish (*deads*),—and the raising of the ore. One of the first objects, therefore, is to cut an *Adit,*† as it is called, which in an in-

---

* The great Copper Mine, called *Crennis,* was discovered by some casual observers in the cliff.

† From *Aditus,* a passage?

clined underground passage, about six feet high,
and $2\frac{1}{2}$ wide, and is generally commenced at the
bottom of a neighbouring valley, and is driven
up to the vein, for the purpose of draining it of
water above their point of contact; these *Adits*
are sometimes continued to a very considerable
distance, and although the expense of forming
them is necessarily very considerable, yet they
are found to afford the most œconomical method
of getting rid of the water, in as much as it saves
the labour of the steam-engine in raising it to
(*Grass*) the surface. As soon as the vertical
aperture, or *Shaft*, is sunk to some depth, a
machine called a *Whim* is erected, to bring up
the *deads*, and ore. It consists of a perpendicular
axis on which a large hollow cylinder of timber,
termed the *Cage*, revolves; and around this a
rope, directed down the *Shaft* by a pulley, winds
horizontally. In the axis a transverse beam is
fixed, at the ends of which two horses are fastened, and going their rounds haul up a basket
(or *Kibbul*) full of ore, or *deads*, whilst an empty
one is descending.* As the lode never runs down
perpendicularly it is necessary to cut galleries,

---

* The application of this machine in the county is estimated as
saving the labour of 10,000 men; whilst the powers of the different steam-engines are considered as at least equivalent to 40,000
more.

called *Levels*, horizontally on the vein, one above
another. These levels are, in the first instance,
about two feet wide, and six feet high, but varying according to circumstances, and being frequently extended much beyond their original dimensions. They are driven one above the other
at intervals of from 10 to 20, or 30 fathoms.
When extended to a certain distance from the
original vertical *Shaft*, it is necessary, for the
sake of ventilation, as well as for other reasons,
to form a second which is made to traverse all
the levels in the same manner as the first. A
communication is frequently only made between
two galleries by a partial shaft (called a *Wins*) in
the interval between the two great shafts. When
there are more than one lode worked in the same
mine, as frequently happens, *Levels* often run
parallel to each other at the same depth. In this
case they communicate by intermediate *Levels*
driven through the rock (or *Country* as it is
called) which are denominated *Cross-cuts*. A
mine thus consists of a series of horizontal galleries, generally one above the other, but sometimes running parallel, traversed at irregular intervals by vertical shafts, and all, either directly
or indirectly, communicating with each other.*

---

* See Dr. Forbes's Paper " On the Temperature of Mines," in
the second volume of the Transactions of the Cornish Society.

The subterranean excavations are effected by breaking down the looser parts by the pickaxe, and by *blasting* the more solid rock by gun· powder.* In accomplishing this latter operation the most melancholy accidents have occurred, in consequence of the iron rammer coming in contact with some siliceous substance, and thus striking fire. The recurrence of this evil it is hoped has been prevented by the laudable efforts of the Geological Society as above related (see page 30), and that the " *Iron Age* " has taken its final departure.

If the traveller is inclined to descend into a mine he is to be first accoutred in a flannel jacket and trowsers, a close cap, an old broad-brimmed hat, and a thick pair of shoes ; a lighted candle is put into one hand, and a spare one suspended to a button of his jacket. The flannel dress is worn close to the skin, in order to absorb the perspiration, and every part of the ordinary dress is laid aside ; thus equipped, if he possess sufficient strength of nerve, he may descend the vertical ladders with the most perfect ease and security ;—but will a view of the mine repay all this trouble and fatigue ?—let us hear what Dr.

---

* The annual cost of gunpowder, used in the mines of the county, amounts to more than thirty thousand pounds.

Forbes has said upon this occasion.* " A person unacquainted with the details of mining, on being informed of many hundreds of men being employed in a single mine, might naturally imagine that a visit to their deep recesses would afford a picturesque and imposing spectacle of gregarious labour and bustle, tremendous noise, and much artificial brilliancy to cheer the gloom. Nothing, however, is further from the truth, as far as regards the mines of Cornwall; for, like their fellow labourers the moles, the miners are solitary in their operations. Seldom do we find more than three or four men in one *level*, or gallery, at a time, where they are seen pursuing the common operations of digging or boring the rock, by the feeble glimmering of a small candle, stuck close by them, with very little noise or much latitude for bodily movement; besides whom there are generally one or two boys employed in wheeling the broken ore, &c. to the shaft. Each of·these boys has also a candle affixed to his wheelbarrow, by the universal subterranean candlestick, a piece of clay. A certain band of men, who, however numerous, are always called " *a Pair*," generally undertake the working of a particular *Level*.

---

* Transactions of the Royal Geological Society of Cornwall, vol. 2, page 162.

These subdivide themselves into smaller bodies, which, by relieving each other at the end of every six or eight hours, keep up the work uninter. ruptedly, except on Sunday. By means of this subdivision of *the Pairs*, there is in general not more than one-third of the underground labourers below at any one time. Very seldom are the miners within the sound of each other's opera- tions, except occasionally when they hear the dull report of the explosions. In the vicinity of the main shaft, indeed, the incessant action of the huge chain of pumps, produces a constant, but not very loud noise, while the occasional rattling of the metallic buckets against the walls of the shaft, as they ascend and descend, relieves the monotony both of the silence and the sound. Still every thing is dreary, dull, and cheerless; and you can be with difficulty persuaded, even when in the richest and most populous mines, that you are in the centre of such extensive and important operations." For keeping the workings from being inundated, each mine is furnished with a chain of pumps, extending from the bottom to the *adit-level*; worked by a single pump-rod; each pump receiving the water brought up by the one immediately below it. All the water of the deep- est level finds its way into the bottom of the mine, technically called the *Sump*, whence it is finally elevated to the adit, through which it flows by a gentle descent to the surface.*

We have yet to notice a fact connected with the natural history of these subterranean recesses, which has lately excited a very considerable share of interest in the members of the Cornish Geological Society,—that *the natural temperature of the earth in these mines is considerably above that of the mean of the climate, and increases with the depth, at the rate of about one degree for every 50 or 60 feet.*† Does there exist then a permanent source of heat in the interior of the earth?

The business of a mine is managed by a foreman, called the *Captain*, who keeps the accounts, and pays and regulates the miners; there are also *Under-ground Captains*, who have the immediate inspection of the works below. There exists a popular belief that the Cornish miner frequently lives under ground for many days, or weeks,

---

* The quantity of water discharged by the pumps from many of the Cornish mines is very considerable; thus *Huel Abraham* discharges from the depth of 1440 feet, about 2,092,320 gallons every 24 hours; *Dolcoath*, from nearly the same depth, 535,173 gallons in the same time; and *Huel Vor*, from the depth of 950 feet, 1,692,660 gallons.

† See Dr. Forbes's paper on the temperature of mines, in the Transactions of the Royal Geological Society of Cornwall, vol. 2, p. 208; also on the temperature of mines, by R.W. Fox, Esq. ibid. p. 14, and a paper on the same subject byM. P. Moyle, Esq. p. 404.

without ever visiting the surface. This is never the case at any time, or under any circumstances. He does not even eat, much less sleep, in the mine, but returns *to grass*, and to his home, often many miles distant, at whatever depth he may have been working, when relieved from his labours.

With respect to the value of the mines, considered as property, it may be observed, that the whole concern is a Lottery, in which there exist many blanks to a prize, and were the whole of the speculation to be invested in any one individual, there is no doubt but that, after paying the required dues to the lords of the soil, and defraying the necessary expenses for working the mines, he would at the conclusion of the year be a loser by many thousand pounds. It is very true that there are many cases of extraordinary gain,* but these are balanced by more numerous concerns in which loss is incurred. How then

---

* Crennis Copper Mine returned a clear profit to the adventurers of £84,000 in one year; and Huel Alfred, during the last period of its working, yielded very nearly £130,000, after having defrayed every necessary expense. The adventurers in Huel Vor have lately gained £10,000 in three months. But, on the contrary, how numerous are the losses, not perhaps corresponding in magnitude, in any individual mine, to the gains which have been above stated. In North Downs as much as £90,000 were lost, but this is a rare instance.

does it happen that any capitalists can be induced to engage in the speculation? the answer is obvious, for the very same reason that they are induced to purchase tickets in the Sate Lottery. There are moreover additional motives which induce individuals of a certain description to embark in the speculation, although, as simple adventurers, they may scarcely anticipate success, such are landholders, who are naturally desirous of promoting an undertaking from which they must necessarily receive considerable dues; or merchants, who by becoming shareholders, are empowered to supply the mines with timber, candles,* gunpowder, and other articles which are required for its working.

Having thus considered the mode in which the ore is excavated from the mine, and brought to the surface, let us examine the processes by which it ultimately assumes the state of marketable metal.

The Tin ore is first *spalled*, as it is termed, that is, broken into smaller fragments, and separated from the worthless parts; it is then pound-

---

* The consumption of such articles in a great mine far exceeds any estimate which a person unacquainted with mining operations could possibly imagine. In *Huel Vor*, no less than Three thousand pounds of candles are consumed in a month, and about Three thousand five hundred pounds of Gunpowder.

ed in the *Stamping mill*,* an operation which is
essential to the complete separation of the oxide
from the hard matrix through which it is disseminated : if full of slime it is first thrown into
a pit called a *buddle*, where it is worked in order
to render the *Stamping* more free, and to prevent
it from choaking the grates ; if however it is free
from slime, the ore is shoveled into a kind of
sloping canal of timber, called the *Pass*, whence
it slides by its own weight, and the assistance of
a small stream of water, into the box where the
Lifters work ; the *Lifters* are raised by a water
wheel, and they are armed at the bottom with
large masses of iron weighing nearly two hundred weight, which pound or *stamp* the ore small
enough for its passage through the holes of an
iron grate fixed in one end of the box, a rill of
water carries it by a small gutter into the *fore
pit*, where it makes its first settlement, the lighter
particles running forward with the water into
the *middle pit*, and thence into the third, where
what is called the *slime*, or finest portion, settles ;
from these pits the ore is carried to the *Keeve*,
which is a large vat containing water, in which

---

* Before the invention of the *Stamping Mill*, the Tin was pulverised in a kind of mortar, called a *Crazing Mill*; one of which
ancient machines is still in the possession of Mr. Williams of Scorrier House.

it is farther purified by an operation called *tozing*, and which consists in stirring the water round by means of a small shovel, with such velocity as to keep the *tin stuff* in a state of suspension, until the whole quantity which can be managed by one operation is thrown into the vat, and when the *Tozer* slackens his efforts, the Tin subsides to the bottom, from its greater specific gravity, leaving the sand and other impurities at the top; while this is going on the upper part of the vessel is beaten with mallets for some minutes, in order more effectually to ensure this separation.

A third process still remains to be described, that of Dressing the sand on an inclined plain with the assistance of a small stream of water; a great degree of manual dexterity is here requisite; the object, however, is effected with less trouble and expense, and much more completely, by the German "*Repercussion Frames*," of which there is a model in the Geological Museum at Penzance.

Upon the same mechanical principle of separation, founded on the relative specific gravities of the Tin oxide, and the earthy matters with which it may be mixed, the Tinner is at once enabled to estimate the value of any given sample of ore; for which purpose the *Tin stuff* is placed on a shovel, and washed under a stream of water, until the impure earthy particles are carried off from its sides, when by a peculiar and dextrous motion, not easily described, all the particles of the ore are collected together on the fore part of the shovel. This operation is called *Vanning.*

When the Tin ore is contaminated with *Mundic,* that is, with *Arsenical* and *Iron Pyrites,* it is first roasted in the *Burning House,* and then washed; by which means the Tin, which is heavy, is easily separated from the other ores, which are comparatively light. If any *Sulphuret of Copper* be present, the same process' is calculated to separate it, by thus converting it into a *Sulphate,** as described at page 128.

When the ore is dressed, the lord of the soil receives that portion which is his due, after which it is divided into as many *doles* or shares, as there are adventurers; and these are measured out by barrows, an account of which is kept, in the manner of the old times, by a person who notches a stick.

The manner of dressing and cleansing *Copper*

---

* This process might be more generally employed in Cornwall with much advantage. The green coloured water which so frequently issues from the adits, might be made to yield a considerable portion of Copper, if it were properly received in pits, and submitted to the action of Iron.

ore is nearly similar to that of Tin, except indeed that as it is raised in large masses, and is tolerably pure, it does not generally require *Stamping*, nor much washing.

All these different processes furnish employment for a great number of women and children, and it is really interesting to see the dexterity and cheerfulness with which they pursue the occupation. There is, however, one practice which ought to be reformed—the burthen of the *Standard Barrow* used in carrying Copper, and which is said to contain three hundred weight; in addition to which we must allow for the weight of the barrow itself, and that of the water held by the recently washed ore, so that it cannot be estimated at less than four hundred weight. This is an enormous burthen, which is borne by all descriptions of persons who are employed in dressing and weighing, and it has given rise to many evils.

Those who work below have generally a wretched and emaciated appearance, although they seldom continue longer under ground than six hours in the twenty-four, but are relieved by a fresh corps. Pulmonary consumption may be said to be the disease to which they are more particularly liable.

N 2

The names by which the Cornish mines are distinguished are usually invented by the first adventurers, and are often whimsical enough, the usual prefix, *Huel*, (always pronounced, and generally erroneously spelt, *Wheel*) signifies in the Cornish language *a hole;* while the specific name of the mine is taken from some trivial or accidental circumstance, thus *Dolcoath* was the name of an old woman, *Dorothy Koath*, who lived upon the spot where the working of the mine commenced; *Huel Providence* was so called from the accidental way in which it was discovered; and *Huel Boys* from the lode having been first noticed by children who had been playing, and digging pits in imitation of shafts.

By a rough calculation it may be stated that there are about 130 mines in the county, but the number is of course subject to variation; old workings being frequently given up, and new mines opened, or forsaken ones resumed.

Besides the mines, there are also " *Stream Works*," which afford a large quantity of the purest *oxide*.* They occur in vallies, and derive their name from the manner in which they are worked; which merely consists in washing the

---

* Stream Tin, on account of its purity, is alone capable of furnishing the *grain tin*, employed principally by dyers.

alluvial soil by directing a stream of water over it, when the finer particles being washed away, the *Tin ore* is procured in a separate form.* The process is termed *Streaming for Tin.* It is a singular fact that the only traces of Gold to be found in Cornwall† are in these alluvial deposi- tions, in which it sometimes occurs in small grains, mostly detached, but occasionally ad- hering to quartz. The miners engaged in the stream works are generally prepared with quills, into which they drop these particles as they find them, and when the quill is full, it is carried to the goldsmith for sale, and considered as a per- quisite.

---

* The principal Stream works are in the parishes of Lanlivery, Luxilian, St. Blazy, St. Austel, St. Mewan, St. Stephens, and St. Columb. The greatest Stream work in the county is at Carnon, about half-way between Truro and Penrhyn; but there is scarcely a valley in which the operation has not been conducted on a small scale.

† In the Ordnance Map of Cornwall, a spot marked " THE GOLD MINE" is noticed, near Liskeard. This name serves only to commemorate one of the many ruinous speculations into which the inhabitants of this County have repeatedly fallen, from a want of mineralogical knowledge. A mass of Pyrites having been dis- covered in this place, its brilliancy induced a belief that it was GOLD, in consequence of which workings were immediately com- menced, and the sanguine adventurers, urged forward no doubt by those who derived an interest from the undertaking, could not be convinced of their error, until the complete ruin of their for- tunes obliged them to abandon every hope.

But it is time for us to resume our topographical descriptions—

In our road to Redruth we pass *Clowance* the seat of Sir John St. Aubyn, Baronet. *Pendarves* the residence of Edward William Wynne Pendarves, Esq. son of the late John Stackhouse, Esq. the elegant author of " *Nereis Britannica,*" and *Tehidy Park*, the mansion of Francis Basset, Lord de Dunstanville, &c.

About two miles west of Redruth, is DOL-COATH, a copper mine which every intelligent traveller ought to visit, not only on account of the immensity of the concern, and the ability and liberality with which it is conducted, but because it is so situated on the brow of a hill, that the spectator can at one glance see all the principal machinery by which it is worked. It is quite impossibe to convey an idea of this singular and interesting scene ;—Steam Engines ;—Water Wheels ; — Horse Whims ; — Stamping Mills,—are all in motion before us, while in the glen beneath us many hundred labourers are to be seen busily engaged in the different operations of separating, dressing, and carrying the ore. The same stream of water pouring down the hill turns successively numerous overshot wheels, and serves various other purposes in its course ;

and, having thus performed upon the surface, all that ingenuity could devise, or the operations of mining require, it is conducted into the bowels of the earth, where, at a hundred and fifty feet beneath its surface, it again turns an overshot wheel of fifty feet in diameter, and becomes again subservient to the skilful exertions of the miner. In the whole circle of human inventions there is nothing which so fully manifests the resources of intellect, for the production of immense effects, as the stupendous art of mining; and it is impossible that the workings of Dolcoath can be viewed without the strongest sensation of wonder and exultation. The works of the mine stretch upwards of a mile in length from east to west; an extent of ground penetrated by innumerable shafts, and honey-combed by subterranean galleries. Upon the summit of the hill is another rich copper mine, *Cook's Kitchen,* which is on the same suite of lodes as *Dolcoath,* but separated by a cross-course which forms a natural boundary to both. This cross-course has so *heaved* the lodes, that many which are worked with great profit in the former mine cannot be discovered in the latter, notwithstanding the laborious search which has been made for that purpose.

The picturesque effect of this scenery is not a little heightened by the bold elevation of *Carn-breh Hill,* which, crowned with the mouldering remains of past ages, rises, as if in mockery of the boasted prowess of art, and forms a most striking and impressive contrast to the active scene before us.

REDRUTH is a very populous town of high antiquity, situated in the bosom of the mining district, and capable of affording very excellent accommodation to the mineralogist who may be desirous of remaining some days for the purpose of inspecting, at his leisure, the numerous mines by which it is surrounded. The general level of this metalliferous district is from 350 to 450 feet above the sea ; and being frequently intersected by vallies, great opportunities are presented for the advantageous construction of *Adits.*

We next proceed to visit the great Steam-Engine of Chacewater mine, situated three miles south of Redruth. It was erected about the year 1813, and was at that period the most powerful machine in the world. It is a double engine upon the improved principle of Bolton and Watt, and the style and elegance with which its different parts are finished, reflect no inconsiderable credit upon the engineer. The following are its dimensions; the cylinder is 66 inches, the box 19, in diameter. The depth of the engine shaft is 128 fathoms. From the *Adit* to the bottom 90 fathoms. It makes eight strokes in a minute, and at every stroke it raises 108 gallons of water to the *Adit;** and, at the same time also, 60 gallons, 10 fathoms high, for the purpose of condensing the steam. The quantity of coals consumed in twenty-four hours is estimated at about eight chaldrons. To give at once a popular idea of its immense power, it may be stated that, if it were applied as a mill, it could grind a Winchester bushel of wheat every minute. Notwithstanding the immensity of its force, and complexity of parts, so completely is it under the discretion and guidance of the engineer, that in one instant he is able to stop its motions by the mere application of his finger and thumb to a screw.—" We put a hook in the nose of the Leviathian;—play with him as a child, and take him as a servant for ever."

From Chacewater we proceed southward about

---

* This is the deepest *Adit* in the country; its mouth or extremity being nearly on a level with the water in one of the creeks of Falmouth Harbour, into which it empties itself. Taking into calculation its various windings, through the numerous mines which it relieves of water, it may be said to be not less than twenty-four miles in length.

two miles to visit the extensive Copper mines, called " *The Consolidated Mines*," the working of which has been lately resumed. Here we shall find two immense Steam Engines, with cylinders of 90 inches in diameter, constantly at work; the interior of which is kept as clean as a drawing-room. The capital expended in setting these mines at work was not less than £65,000, and under the arrangement of Mr. William Davey, the concern has proved so profitable, that shares are now selling in London at £100 per cent. profit.

Near the *Consolidated Mines* are *Huel Unity* and *Poldice*; the former is a Copper mine; the latter produces both Copper and Tin. The most beautiful specimens of *Arseniate of Copper*, and *Arseniate of Lead* have been found in these mines.

Having concluded our account of the mining district, it remains for us to offer to the minera-logical tourist a few observations upon the subject of Cornish Minerals, and upon the best method of procuring them; before the stranger, however, attempts to purchase any specimens, it will be well for him to inspect the several splendid cabinets in the county; besides that in the museum of the Royal Geological Society,

at Penzance, he should see those in the possession of William Rashleigh, Esq. M. P. of *Menabilly ;* John Williams, Esq. of *Scorrier House,*
and Joseph Carne, Esq. of *Penzance.* The one
in possession of Mr. Rashleigh, if not the most
accessible to the mineralogist, must be confessed
to be without comparison, the most splendid. Its
chief excellence consists in the magnificence and
variety of the *Oxide of Tin,†* *Fluors, Malachite,*
and some of the rarer varieties of *Sulphuret of
Copper,* from mines which have long since ceased
to be worked. Among the more remarkable
specimens are those of *Oxide of Tin* (from Saint
Agnes) some of the more interesting varieties of
which present the following forms,—very large
octohedrons with, and without, truncations ;—
the crystal described by Klaproth as one of the
rarest occurrence, *viz.* — the four-sided prism,
with a four-sided pyramid at each extremity ;
this is to be seen in its simple form, and also
with a rich variety of truncations ;—a group of
four-sided pyramids covered with a thin coating

---

* Menabilly is situated about four miles west of Fowey, on an
eminence at a short distance from the sea.

† We have been told that this has been arranged by Mr. Aikin,
according to the different modifications of its crystalline form, as
they are described by Mr. William Phillips in his elaborate paper
published in the 2nd Vol. of the Transactions of the London
Geological Society.

of *Calcedony*, which, being *hydrophanous*, shews the form of the crystal very distinctly after immersion in water; *Wood-tin* forming a vein in a matrix of quartz, to one side of which adheres a fragment of rock; it is hardly necessary to remind the mineralogist of the importance of this specimen in a geognostic point of view;* Tin crystals having a coating of black *hæmatite*; *Sulphuret of Tin*, a mineral which has never been found in any part of the world except at *Huel Rock*, in Saint Agnes, *Stenna-gwyn*, in Saint Stephen's, and *Huel Scorrier* in Gwennap.† In the collection of Tins may be seen several small blocks‡ of that metal, as prepared by the Jews, for commerce, during the early workings of the Cornish mines, among which is a fraudulent one consisting of a mass of stone covered with a thin coating of metal. In the collection of Coppers may be noticed *Yellow*

---

* See an interesting account of this mineral in a notice entitled " Contributions towards a knowledge of the Geological History of Wood-Tin, by A. Majendie, Esq." in the first volume of the Transactions of the Royal Geological Society of Cornwall.

† Since the first edition of this work was printed, the mineral has been found at *Saint Michael's Mount*, and, by Dr. Boase, amongst a pile of ore which was supposed to come from *Botallack*.

‡ In one of which is to be seen the *Muriate of Tin*, as first noticed by the late Reverend William Gregor.

Copper ore with *Opal* (from Roskeir); *the triple Sulphuret of Antimony, Copper, and Lead* in various forms; *Ruby Copper* in cubes; *Quartz* containing globules of water; the *Hydrargyllite* or *Wavellite,* in a plumose form accompanied by *Apatite* in a matrix of Quartz (from Saint Stephen's), *Topazes* of considerable lustre (from Saint Agnes), *Green Fluor* in crystals of twenty-four sides (Saint Agnes). A most beautiful and instructive cube of *Fluor,* the surface of which reflects a delicate green hue, but upon being held to the light the crystal exhibits its octohedral nucleus of a purple colour. The mineralogist should also notice a superb octohedron *of Gold,* and a mass of *Stalactitical Arragonite* from the grotto of Antiparos. Before quitting Menabilly he ought to visit the grotto, built in a beautiful and secluded part of the grounds, near the shore in the port of Polredmouth. It stands at the extremity of a large grove, and is constructed with the finest species of marble and serpentine, with brilliant crystals, pebbles, and shells; its form is that of an octagon, two of the sides of which are appropriated to the door and window which front each other, while the six remaining sides form receptacles for minerals, four of which contain specimens of ores found in the county, and two are filled with organic fossils, polished agates, and jaspers; the intermediate spaces are occupied by shells, coralloids, and various other substances. The roof is composed of *Stalactites* of singular beauty, and which produce a very striking effect as they are seen through the roughly formed arch which composes the entrance. In this grotto are preserved two links of the chain which were found in Fowey harbour by some fishermen in the year 1776; they are of a triangular form, incrusted with shells and corals, and are supposed to have formed a part of the chain which extended from tower' to tower, for the ancient defence of the harbour. Among the mineralogical specimens in this place there is one of *Calcedony* which deserves particular notice for its beauty as well as magnitude. In the centre of the grotto is a table inlaid with thirty-two polished specimens of granite, all found in the county of Cornwall.

THE CABINET OF JOHN WILLIAMS, ESQ. is at Scorrier House, about two miles east of Redruth, and may therefore be visited by the mineralogist in the present excursion. This collection stands unrivalled in the magnificence of its specimens of *Red Oxide of Copper*, in octohedrons, cubes, and capillary crystals; it also contains the finest specimens of *Arseniate of Copper* in very perfect obtuse octohedrons ;—a mass of *Uranite,* which in size and beauty is superior to any specimens ever discovered;—*Blende,* in octohedrons and cubes ;—*Native, and Ruby Silver*; and a specimen of the *Muriate* of that metal (*Horn Silver*) so well known for its value, that it may be said to constitute one of the most interesting objects in the collection. The *Arseniate of Lead,* in six-sided prisms, a most beautiful mineral, which was first analysed by Mr. Gregor, and has been found only in *Huel Unity,* may be seen in this cabinet in its most perfect forms.

The collection of Mr. Carne has been already noticed in our account of Penzance, at *page 31.*

In order to collect the various minerals of the county the stranger must apply to the different dealers,* (*rapax et sordidum pecus*) and make the best bargain he is able; he may also occasionally purchase some good specimens of the miners at the various mines he may happen to visit. In his rambles we recommend him to visit Saint

---

* The following are the names of the respectable dealers to whom we recommend the mineralogist to apply,—At *Truro,* Tregoning, Mudge, and Heard ;—at *Redruth,* Bennett; at. *Gwenap,* Michell ;—at *Saint Agnes,* Argall ;—at *Falmouth,* Trathan ;—and at *Penzance,* Jacobs, the latter of whom has generally a great variety of Saint Just minerals on sale.

Agnes, where are the *Trevaunance,* and *Seal Hole* mines, from which have been raised the most beautiful specimens of crystallized Tin in the world, accompanied occasionally with *Topazes,* and twenty-four-sided *Fluor.* Here too may be seen a geological phenomenon of considerable interest,—the slate of the coast intersected with *Porphyry Dykes.* Saint Agnes' Beacon is also well worthy of observation; it is an insulated eminence of a pyramidal form, entirely covered with *debris,* and is composed of *Slate,* although it rises 664 feet above the level of the sea. Saint Agnes is the birth place of the celebrated artist Opie,* and the tourist may be gratified by inspecting many of the earlier productions of his pencil. But we now take our leave of the Mineralogist, and shall attend the Antiquary in order to inspect *Carn-breh hill,* which rises a little to the south-west of Redruth, to an elevation of 697 feet; its principal interest is

---

* Opie was a parish apprentice to a person of the name of Wheeler, a house carpenter, in the village of Saint Agnes; Dr. Walcott, better known by his poetical appellation of *Peter Pindar,* having been struck, during his occasional visits to the village, by some rude sketches in chalk which were shewn him as the productions of this poor lad, invited him to his house at *Truro,* supplied him with the necessary materials, and enabled him to set up as an itinerant portrait painter, from which station he rose to be Professor of Painting to the Royal Academy.

derived from the lucubrations of Dr. Borlase, who regarded it as having been the grand centre of Druidical worship, and he asserts that, in his time, the remains of the monuments which were peculiar to that priesthood were to be easily recognized, such as *Rock Basins*; *Circles*; *Crom-lechs*; *Rock Idols*; *Karns*; *Caves*; *religious enclosures*; *Logan Stones*; a *Gorseddau*, or place of elevation, whence the Druids pronounced their decrees; and the traces of a *Grove of Oaks!*— this is all very ingenious and imposing, but is there any rational testimony in support of such an hypothesis? are there any just grounds for considering the objects to which he alludes as the works of art?—most certainly none, they are unquestionably the results of the operation of time and the elements, and have never been formed by any agents except those which Nature employs in the decomposition of granitic masses; but the age of Antiquarian illusion is past; the light of geological science dispels the phantoms which the wizard fancy had created, just as the rising sun dissolves the mystic forms which the most common object assumes in twilight, when viewed through the medium of credulity and superstition. The *rock basins* of Antiquaries are rounded cavities on the surface of rocks, and are

o

occasionally as spheroidal, internally, as if they had been actually shaped by a turning lathe; it was this artificial appearance which first suggested the hypothesis concerning their origin, and induced the Antiquary to regard them as pools of lustration. Dr. Mac Culloch,[*] however, very justly observes, that their true nature is very easily traced by inspecting the rocks themselves; on examining the excavations they will be always found to contain distinct grains of *Quartz*, and fragments of the other constituent parts of the granite; a small force is sufficient to detach from the sides of these cavities additional fragments, shewing beyond doubt, that a process of decomposition is still going on under favourable circumstances; these circumstances are the presence of water, or rather the alternate action of air and moisture; if a drop of water can only make an effectual lodgement on a surface of this granite a small cavity must be sooner or later produced, this insensibly enlarges as it becomes capable of holding more water, and the sides as they continue to waste necessarily retain an even and rounded cavity, on account of the uniform

---

[*] A highly interesting paper " On the decomposition of the Granite Tors of Cornwall," by this geologist, is published in the second volume of the Transactions of the Geological Society of London.

texture of the granite. This explanation is sufficiently satisfactory; in addition to which it may be further stated, that these very *basins* not unfrequently occur on the perpendicular sides of rocks,* which at once excludes the idea of their artificial origin.

The other grotesque and whimsical appearances of rocky masses, such as " *rock idols, logan stones,*" &c. are to be explained upon the tendency which granite possesses of wearing more rapidly on the parts which are most exposed to the action of the weather, as already explained at page 104. There occurs upon the western part of the ridge of *Carn-breh* an equipoised stone, about 20 feet in diameter, affording a very singular illustration of these views, and of which we shall here present a sketch to our readers.

* This may be distinctly seen in the granitic rocks in the islands of Scilly; and in the *Gritstone* in the park of the late Sir Joseph Banks, in the parish of Ashover in Derbyshire.

Thus upon simple and philosophical principles are such appearances to be easily explained, and this *Phantasmagoria* of the learned antiquary vanishes.

For the information of the Geologist who may visit this spot, we shall state, that in a porphyritic granite on the summit, Mr. W. Phillips has lately discovered that some of the crystals formerly considered as *Felspar*, were *Cleavelandite*;* and we have little doubt that this curious discovery might be extended to many of the granitic masses in Western Cornwall.

At the eastern end of the hill is *Carn-breh Castle*; the rocks upon which this building stands, not being contiguous, are connected by arches turned over the cavities; one part of the fortress pierced with loop holes is evidently very ancient, and is supposed to have been of British work; the other is of modern construction, and was probably erected as an ornamental object from the grounds of Tehidy. There were formerly

---

* The only chemical difference between *Cleavelandite* and *Felspar* is, that about 12 per cent. of Potass in the latter is replaced by an equal quantity of Soda in the former. The earthy ingredients in both minerals are the same, and exist in similar proportions. The primary form of each is a doubly oblique prism, but the two prisms differ so essentially from each other in the measurement of their angles, that the substances are easily distinguished from each other by the Goniometer.

some outworks to the north-west; and, near the summit of the hill is a circular fortification called the *Old Castle*, which appears to have been included within a strong wall. The hill itself, on which the spectator stands, is quite in unison with the scene around him; its silence and desolation,—the awful vestiges of its convulsion,—and the immense rocky fragments which lie scattered on its brow, are well calculated to harmonize with an extended and barren tract of country, every where broken up by mining operations, and whose horizon is bounded by the ocean.

EXCURSION VI.

TO KYNANCE COVE, AND THE LIZARD POINT.

——

An excursion to the peninsula of the Lizard offers to the scientific traveller many objects of great geological interest; he will be enabled to examine a very rare and important series of Rock Formations, while their various gradations and transitions into each other will afford ample materials for speculation. In the course of this excursion it will be our duty to point out some of the more prominent features as they may occur in our progress; but in performing this duty we wish to be considered as merely presenting the geologist with a rough and imperfect outline, which may give a useful direction to his researches, and enable him to acquire, through the medium of his own observation, more ample and perfect information. *

———

* Before his departure upon this excursion, we recommend him to examine the very instructive suite of specimens which were col-

To the country south of a line drawn from the mouth of the Helford river, on the east, to the Loe-Bar on the west, has the appellation of the " *Lizard District*" been exclusively applied by Mr. Majendie ; and the division appears to have been conventionally received by all the geologists who have traced his steps.

The fundamental rock of this peninsula appears to be *Clay-slate*, associated with *Greywacké*, upon which are successively deposited *Greenstone, Diallage rock,* and *Serpentine.* At Marazion several alternate beds of *Slate* and *Greenstone* may be observed; the latter of which contains *Asbestus-Actynolite,* and is universally traversed by veins of *Axinite*,* which occurs both in an amorphous and crystalline form.

lected, and deposited in the Cabinet at Penzance by *Mr. Ashhurst Majendie,* a gentleman whose geological labours in this country are well known, and whose zeal and ability so greatly promoted the early advancement of our Geological Society. This valuable series has been greatly augmented by a Collection since presented to the Society by *The Reverend John Rogers.* The Geological tourist ought at the same time to make himself acquainted with the observations of *Mr. Majendie* " *On the Lizard District,*" in the first volume of the Transactions of the Royal Geological Society of Cornwall ; and those of *Mr. Professor Sedgwick,* on the same subject, in the Transactions of the Cambridge Philosophical Society.

* In the *Greeb-rock,* an insulated mass of greenstone in the sea beneath, there is a vein of *Asbestus-Actynolite,* mixed with *Axinite,* from four to twelve inches wide. This is a curious spot, well worthy the attention of the geologist.

In the vicinity of a projecting ledge of rocks, known by the name of *Cuddan Point,* stands a mansion called *Acton Castle,* which was erected as a marine residence by the late John Stackhouse, Esq. and is at present occupied by Capt. Praed. Its situation is wild and unsheltered, but it commands a prospect of very extraordinary grandeur and beauty.

About four miles from Marazion, and half a mile from the high road towards the coast, are the remains of a building called *Pengerswick Castle,* a square stone tower, with a smaller one annexed, and some ruins of walls, are all that remain of this ancient edifice, but its machiolated gate and embattled turrets are still preserved to announce its military origin. The different rooms are now converted into granaries, but the oak wainscot, which is curiously carved and painted, remains in a tolerable state of preservation. On one of these pannels, under a rude representation of water dropping from a rock, with the title " *Perseverance,*" is the following poetical inscription.

> " What thing is harder than a rock?
>   What softer is than water clear?
> Yet will the same with often drop
>   The hard rock pierce, which doth appear,
> Even so there's nothing so hard to attayne
> But may be had with labour and pain."

The classical reader will at once recognise in this inscription a paraphrase of the well known lines of Ovid:

" Quid magis est saxo durum,—Quid mollius unda?
Dura tamen molli Saxa cavantur Aqua."

There exists a tradition that this place belonged in the reign of Henry VIII. to one Milliton, who having slain a man privately, purchased the castle in the name of his son, and immured himself in a secret chamber in the tower.

On a bold pile of *Granite rocks* which projects from the shore near Pengerswick, Dr. Maton observed clusters of *Trochus crassus,* besides some species of *Actinia* and *Asterias,* not common on other parts of the coast. Pursuing our route we pass through a country principally composed of Slate, the great Granite chain running to the left of the road, and constituting *Tregoning,* *Godolphin,* and *Breage hills.* The Signal house at the top of *Tregoning hill,* which is 584 feet above the sea, constitutes the most elevated point in the country, and from which both channels are visible. The granite of this hill bears in some parts all the appearance of a stratified rock.

Upon arriving at the village of *Breage*, three miles west of Helston, the traveller should turn off from the high road, in order to visit the Tin Mine called *Huel Vor*, and which lies about a mile and a half to the north-east, and is by far the largest as well as the richest Tin Mine ever worked in Cornwall. Here there are five large Steam Engines for drawing the water out of the mine, besides several others for raising the ore. There are also four large Stamping Mills, worked by Steam, which constitute by far the most interesting part of the machinery. It is not many years since steam was first applied as the moving power of these mills, but without its aid it would have been impossible to stamp the whole of *Huel Vor* Tin with sufficient expedition. In this mine all the operations are carried on which have been already described in our excursion to Redruth, and the Mining Districts. The ore is also roasted and smelted on the spot. Here then the stranger may witness the whole process, from the period when the ore is broken in the vein, to that when the pure Tin runs out of the furnace, and is laded into moulds which contain about 370 pounds. The principal Tin *lode* in this mine is, in one part, of the enormous width of 30 feet, and is so rich withal, that the adventurers lately gained a clear profit of upwards of £10,000, in the space of three months. The workings extend for more than a mile and a quarter under ground, and about thirteen hundred persons are engaged in conducting its operations.

On the Coast, about three miles west of Helston, is Portleven harbour; notwithstanding the enormous sum of money which has been expended in completing this work, we believe that it is never likely to answer the object for which it was projected; the fact is simply this, that at those times when the severity of the weather renders such a refuge desirable to the navigators of the Mount's Bay, the sea sets in with such tremendous force upon this part of the coast that it is absolutely unsafe for any vessels to approach it, and still more so to attempt a passage into the basin, through its narrow entrance.

HELSTON is a large and populous town, containing nearly 3000 inhabitants, situated on the side of a hill which slopes gradually to the little river *Cober*. The houses are chiefly disposed in four streets in the form of a cross, and, at the point of intersection, stand the market house and town hall. The church, which was erected A.D. 1762, at the sole expense of the then Earl of Godolphin, stands on an eminence to the north, and forms a very pleasing object from the valley below, while to the tempest tossed mariner it serves as a useful landmark.

Helston has returned members to Parliament ever since Edward I., being one of the five ancient boroughs of Cornwall. There was formerly a castle, on the site of the present bowling green, but of which no vestige remains. The town is now lighted by means of gas.

In this town we shall be gratified to find the traces of an ancient custom, which the Antiquary has been anxious to trace to so high a source as the Roman *Floralia*, a festival observed by that people, in honour of the Goddess Flora, on the fourth of the Calends of May. It is called the *Furry*, and it is said that its present name alone would discover its origin, were it not satisfactorily pointed out by the time of its celebration. We confess ourselves to have been amongst the happy number* who regarded the annual festival of Helston as a faint trace of the Roman *Floralia* which the abrasion of fourteen centuries had not wholly obliterated. But the evil genius of Reality has at length appeared to dispel the illusion,

---

* As will appear on the perusal of the first edition of this little work.

and to extort from us the unwilling belief that it can be no other than the anniversary of a victory, obtained by the natives over an invading enemy.

The morning of the *Eighth of May* is ushered in with the sound of drums and kettles, when the streets are soon thronged with spectators, and assistants in the *Mysteries*. So strict is the observance of this day as a general holiday, that should any person be found at work, he is instantly seized, set astride on a pole, and hurried on men's shoulders to the river, where, if he does not commute his punishment by a fine, he is sentenced to leap over a wide place, which he of course fails in attempting, and falls into the water, to the great amusement of the spectators. At about the hour of nine the revellers appear before the Grammar school, and make their demand of a prescriptive holiday, after which they collect contributions from house to house. They then *fadé* into the country (*fadé* being an old English word for *go*), and about noon return with flowers and oak branches in their hats and caps; from this time they dance, hand in hand, through the streets, preceded by a violin,* play-

---

* A violiu is in some parts of Cornwall called a *Crowd*, whence doubtless the name of *Crowdero*, the fiddler in Hudibras.

ing an ancient traditional tune, the music of
which we shall here introduce.

There is also a traditional song which is sung
in chorus, involving the history of Robin-Hood,
whose connection with the present festival it is
not easy to understand.

Upon this occasion it is a right, assumed from
time immemorial, for the persons engaged in the
dance to enter and run through any house they
please, without molestation.

The higher classes of the inhabitants having,
with much good humour, assisted in the rites of
the day, and performed their *exforensic* orgies,
resort to the ball room, where they are usually
met by the neighbouring families, and by those
strangers who may happen to be in this part of
Cornwall. The merry dance is commenced at

an early hour, and generally protracted to the dawn of the ensuing day.

Long may this harmless and innocent festival continue to animate the blythe and young, on each annual return of its celebration;—Its classic spell may be dissolved, but the Temple of Hilarity, consecrated by the smiles of Cornish youth and beauty, needs not a Roman goddess for its sanction.

> Why ask where the Flora derives its gay birth!
>   Why each smiling brow wears its garland to-day?
> Enough that our sires kept it sacred to mirth,
>   And their children have hearts all as fervent as they.
>
> And yet might we trace where his ashes are laid
>   Who first made the *Fadé* to sound in our bowers,
> To-day round his cromlech the dance should we braid,
>   And the fairest of Hellas * enwreath it with flowers.
>
> And hallow'd for aye be their place of repose,
>   Who their race have enrich'd with a dowry so rare,
> A spell—that yet brightens each year as it flows
>   With one gleam of Eden—a day free from care.
>
> Then join we the Dance! to their mem'ries of yore,
>   Let the mirth which they lov'd be the homage we pay.
> And the strain that inspir'd them long ages before,
>   Wake the joys, which they felt, in our bosoms to-day.

About two miles from Helston is *Penrose*, the seat of John Rogers, Esq. situated in the midst of a finely wooded scene, and on the border of a

---

* The ancient name of Helston. The modern apellation is derived from a huge block of Granite which may be seen in the yard of the Angel Inn—*Hellas-stone*, or *Helston*.

large sheet of water called the *Loe Pool*; this forms one of the most considerable lakes in the county, and is produced by a very singular operation of nature,—the continual rolling of the waves of the British Channel towards the shore forces in a vast quantity of sand and pebbles, which, by constant accumulation, at length forms a very high bank extending across the valley, from hill to hill, and by closing up the mouth of the channel occasions the river to spread its waters over an area of nearly seven miles in circumference. This bar of gravel cannot be passed over by the waves of the highest tides, even during the excitement of a storm, unless it be attended with a very rare combination of circumstances. The water of the lake gradually finds its way through the gravel of the bar by slow filtration ; but in wet seasons, as it cannot pass off with a rapidity equal to its influx, the lake will often rise ten feet higher than its ordinary level. This produces the singular effect of stopping two mills, one on the *Loe*, the other on a lateral stream, their wheels being at this time partly under water. When this occurs the millers present the Lord of the Manor with two leathern purses, each containing three halfpence, and solicit his permission to open a passage through the bar.

This being of course granted, the Mayor of Helston engages workmen to carry the work into effect. In a few days, however, the bar is again filled up as before.

The *Loe Pool* abounds with a peculiar trout, and other fresh-water fish. On its banks the Botanist may gather *Corrigiola Littoralis*.

In proceeding to the Lizard Point, which is about fourteen miles distant from Helston, we shall examine the line of coast south of the Loe bar. The interior of this peninsular region has an aspect of dreary and barren uniformity, and when viewed from the high granite ridge near Constantine, it appears like a table land elevated some hundred feet above the level of the sea, presenting hardly any indication of rupture or contortion throughout the whole extent of its outline. The view of the same region from the western shore of the Mount's Bay is still more striking and characteristic; the upper surface seems so exactly horizontal, that one might almost be led to conjecture, that every projecting ledge had been planed down until the promontory resembled a great artificial terrace.*

---

* On the physical structure of the Lizard district, by the Rev. A Sedgwick.

Near *Gunwalloe Cove* the geologist should notice the singularly contorted appearance of the
slaty rock, which continues as far as a small cove
north of *Mullion*, called *Bolerium*, where it
runs under a *Greenstone* composed of *Hornblende*
and *Compact Felspar*. The *Greenstone* prevails
through the whole of this district, and appears to
pass by a slow gradation into *Serpentine*, under
which it lies, as may be distinctly seen near the
south side of *Mullion Cove*.* A small quantity
of *Diallage* is occasionally present in this rock,
but the predominant ingredient is common *Hornblende*; and where this latter substance greatly
predominates over the *Felspar*, it in some places
assumes an earthy appearance and decomposes
into a kind of *Clay*, which is used in the neighbourhood with excellent effect as a top dressing
for grass lands.

Serpentine is the next formation which we discover in our progress, and is that which confers
such singular interest upon this part of the county, since it occurs in no other part of England.
This beautiful rock derives its name from the
variegated colours and spots, supposed to resem-

---

* The same relative position of these rocks may also be observed
at *Cadgwith*, an interesting part of the coast north-east of the Lizard
Point, and which we shall have occasion to notice hereafter.

ble the speckles of a serpent's skin; it is principally of a dark green or brown, suffused with shades of red. It occupies not less than one-third of the area of the peninsula; the whole extent of *Goonhilly downs* rests on it. Its boundary is easily traced, says *Mr. Sedgwick,* by the brown scanty vegetation with which its surface is imperfectly covered; and the Professor might have added, by the growth of that beautiful heath, the *Erica Vagans,* for so congenial and essential would a Magnesian soil appear to its production, that notwithstanding its immense profusion on the downs, not a single specimen is to be found beyond the line which defines the boundary of the *Serpentine* formation, nor is it to be seen in any other part of England. *Genista Anglica* is also to be found on these downs.

About three miles south of Mullion, close to the shore, is the celebrated *Steatite,* or *Soap Rock,* which appears to run in veins* in the Ser-

* Sir H. Davy, in a paper on the Geology of Cornwall, published in the first volume of our Transactions, observes that " the nature and origin of the veins of *Steatite* in Serpentine are curious subjects of inquiry. Were they originally crystallized, and the result of chemical deposition ? Or have they been, as for the most part they are now found, mere mechanical deposites, I am inclined to the last opinion. The *Felspar* in Serpentine is very liable to decompose, probably from the action of Carbonic acid and water

pentine, although Dr. Thomson is inclined to consider it as Serpentine itself in a state of decomposition. When it is first quarried it is soft, but by exposure to air it gradually hardens, although it never loses that peculiar *soapy* feel which characterises it. Dillwyn & Co. of Swansea have, at present, the works in their possession, by paying to the proprietor, Lord Falmouth, a certain annual sum. Its value in the manufacture of China depends upon its infusibility, and the property it possesses of retaining its colour in the heat of the furnace; the first quality is to be explained by the total absence of lime in its composition, the latter by the very small proportion of metallic matter contained in it. There is, moreover, another purpose which it serves, depending upon the peculiar property of *Magnesian earth* in preventing that degree of contraction* which always occurs in the fire when *Alumina* and *Silica* are alone made use of. Near this spot veins of *Native Copper* may be fre-

---

on its Alkaline, Calcareous, and Magnesian elements; and its parts washed down by water, and deposited in the chasms of the rocks, would necessarily gain that kind of loose aggregation belonging to Steatite."

* It might on this account be worth while for the Glass-maker to try the effects of a small mixture of *Steatite* with the materials of which he makes his large crucibles, in order to prevent that great degree of shrinking to which they are now so liable.

quently seen at low water during spring tides, and a mass of this metal was once raised which weighed 104 pounds. Copper is the only metallic substance that has been found in any quantity in the Serpentine formation; and this has never occurred except *native*, as in the above instance, or in the state of *Green Carbonate*, so that the mining adventurer need not anticipate much advantage from it.

About a mile farther south is KYNANCE COVE, justly celebrated as one of the most interesting and extraordinary spots on the coast; the descent into it is extremely steep, and overhung with frowning crags; the cove itself is formed by a numerous assemblage of Serpentine rocks of a dark colour, and which exhibit a beautiful polish from the constant attrition of the waves at high water; in one part, these groups are so singularly disposed as to open a fine natural arch into a grotto, which penetrates deeply into the cliff; the largest of these pyramidal masses is termed the ASPARAGUS ISLAND, from its being the habitat of *Asparagus Officinalis*. One of the rocks in this cove exhibits a very curious phenomenon whimsically called the DEVIL'S BELLOWS; there is a very deep chasm, through which the sea rushes like a water spout, preceded by a

submarine rumbling, as loud as thunder; a flow-
ing tide, accompanied with a swell of the waves,
seems to be essential for the production of this
effect. De Luc offers the following explanation
of the phenomenon; " In the rock there is a
succession of caverns, into which the agitated sea
rushes by some sub-marine passage, and being
dashed and broken against their sides, a large
quantity of air* is thus disengaged from them,
which becoming highly compressed, and not
being able to escape beneath, in consequence of
the perpetual entrance of the waves, is forced to
pass with great violence and noise from cavern
to cavern, until it forces itself, together with a
column of water, through the opening above."
Amongst these beautiful rocks may be seen *Diallage* of a brown colour; *Jade*; *compact Felspar,*
or *Saussurite*; and *Asbestus*. *Dykes of Felspar
Porphyry* are also to be observed in this spot.
It is hardly necessary to inform the geological
tourist that, in order to view this interesting
scene to his satisfaction, he must contrive to
arrive at a period near that of low water.

---

* The quantity of air thus separated from water is so great that
in the Alps and in the Pyrennees, very powerful bellows are made
for forges by the fall of a column of water, through a wooden pipe,
into a closed cask, in which it dashes on a stone in the bottom,
when the air thus disengaged from it is carried by another pipe
placed in the cover of the cask into the foundery.

On the summit of the hill above this cove the Botanist will observe *Geranium Sanguineum* spreading itself in broad tufts. *Campanula Rotundifolia* also occurs here.

Continuing our route towards Cape Lizard, we shall perceive that the *Serpentine* terminates about half a mile before we reach it, and is succeeded by *Micaceous Slate*, under which, at the Lizard head lie alternate beds of *Compact Felspar*, containing specks of *Hornblende* and *green Talc*. There are two light-houses at this point which front the south, and stand nearly abreast of each other, but unhappily they are too often found to be insufficient securities against the darkness of the midnight storm, and the treachery of the sunken rocks with which this stern coast is beset. Foreign pilots, unacquainted with its perils, seldom keep the necessary distance from the shore, and from the steepness of the rocks no kind of assistance can be afforded to the mariner from the land.

On a low hedge under the light-houses is to be found *Herniaria Glabra*. It was here in the pursuit of this very plant that a well known Botanist, during the late war, was seized as a spy by the suspicious natives, and carried to Helston for examination. The increased intercourse, however, with scientific travellers, will render the recurrence of such an event impossible.

The name of the promontory was most proba· bly derived from the striking *contour* which it exhibits when viewed from sea, resembling the elongated and compressed form of the Lizard; at the same time it must be observed, that the colour of its rocks resemble also that of the animal to which we allude, while the British words *Lis-ard* signify a lofty projection; these are extraordinary coincidences, and are well calculated to fan the flame of etymological controversy.

If after visiting this promontory, the traveller feels inclined to trace the different rock formations, and to complete his geological survey of the Lizard *Chersonesus*, we recommend him to return by a circuitous route along its eastern coast. *Greenstone* reappears about half a mile east of the Lizard Point, and continues for some distance, with the occasional interruption of Serpentine, which dips towards the sea. This latter rock will be found best adapted for œconomical purposes at the *Balk Hill, Landewednock*, but it is certainly far inferior to that worked for chimney pieces, columns, &c. from the quarries in the Isle of Anglesea. Near *Cadgwith* the rocks on the coast form a very interesting and extraordinary amphitheatre, which is termed by the inhabitants the FRYING PAN, although the appellation of CAULDRON, which it strongly resembles, would be much more appropriate. Its sides are nearly two hundred feet in height, and, at high water, the sea enters it and boils up through an arch near its bottom. In this spot the position of the *Serpentine* upon *Greenstone* is very apparent. Beyond *Cadgwith* the *Serpentine* assumes a dark green colour, and contains small masses of the emerald green *Diallage*, or *Schiller-spar;* whence it continues to constitute the coast round the *Black Head* to *Coverack Cove.* About a mile from the coast at *Gwenter*, the rock denominated by Abbe Haüy " *Diallage Rock*" *(Gabbro)* presents itself to our notice ; it is composed of *Saussurite*, or *Compact Felspar*, and *Diallage Metalloide.* In a quarry near this spot it may be seen to join *Serpentine.* In the *Diallage Rock*, at a small village near the coast called *Gwendra*, as well as in the rock of *Saint Keverne*, Mr. Majendie discovered some small metallic specks, which he found on chemical examination to consist of Iron, with a portion of *Titanium*. Some of the same substance was immediately transmitted to Mr. William Gregor, who stated that the results of his experiments proved it to be an assemblage of several ingredients, *viz. Silica, Alumina,* and the *Oxides of Iron* and *Titanium,* with a little *Potass.* Some of which ingredients were no doubt derived from the *gangue* with which the metallic substance is intimately mixed. This is a discovery no less curious than important, and would seem to point out the origin of the *Menachanite,* in which *Titanium* was first discovered by Mr. Gregor.

The great mass of *Serpentine* ends at *Coverack Cove,* a spot which well deserves the attention of the Geologist, as offering a series of rocks of a very mixed character; these consist of green and reddish-brown *Serpentine,* with the *Jade* of Saussure, (the *feldspath tenace* of Haüy) and *Diallage* * of the green and metalloïde varieties; some of the *Felspar* found here is of a violet colour, and is striated like that of Labrador. In beds which lie below high-water mark in this Cove the mineralogist may obtain masses of *Diallage Metalloïde,* six or eight inches in

---

* This substance presents with great distinctness those characters which distinguish it from *Hornblende,* viz. inferior hardness, difficult fusibility into a green enamel, and peculiar cleavage which discovers a considerable lustre in one direction which is entirely absent in the other; whereas *Hornblende* has natural joints of the same lustre in two directions.

length.+ A beautiful rock succeeds and continues for three miles along the coast to the
Manacles; and in the interior of the country it
predominates through the greater part of the
parish of *Saint Keverne.* It has *compact Felspar*
for its base, in which are imbedded crystals both
of *Diallage* and *Hornblende.* In the proportion,
as well as the magnitude of these constituents,
says Mr. Professor Sedgwick, there is such an
unusual variety, that we were almost led to
conjecture, that during the deposition of the
mass many conflicting principles had been in
action, not one of which was long able to keep
the mastery over the others; there are for instance many large blocks which in one part
resemble a fine *Greenstone,* and in another, a
coarse porphyritic *Diallage Rock*; within the
distance of a few feet these varieties may be
observed to alternate repeatedly, sometimes in
the form of stripes, but more frequently in amorphous concretions separated from each other by

---

+ Mr. Majendie presented some of these specimens to Abbe
Haüy, and compared them with those in the cabinet of that
illustrious mineralogist, which were brought from the hill of
Mussinet near Turin. M. Haüy observed upon this occasion, that
the *Coverack* Specimens did not consist of pure *Diallage,* but that
fibres of common *Hornblende* interrupted its texture. That of
Mussinet is foliated, and has no such intermixture.

lines which are perfectly defined. *Schistose Greenstone* occurs again at *Porthowstock*, and a small bed of *Serpentine*, on the south-west side of *Porthallo* in the cliff, which rests on a reddish *Talc* which lies, as before, on *Clay Slate.* No other variety is observable from hence to the Helford River, except in the appearance of a *Pudding Stone*, or *Conglomerate*, near the *Dennis Creek*, composed of rounded fragments of Slate in which veins of *Quartz* are distinctly visible. The traveller will not fail to visit the stream of *Tregonwell Mill*,* near the village of *Menacchan*, celebrated as the habitat of the *Titaniferous Iron (Menacchanite*, or *Gregorite)* discovered by the late celebrated Mr. William Gregor.† He will also receive much gratification by extending his route to *Mawnan* Cliffs, where he will observe a most extraordinary intermixture of fine and coarse grained *(Grawacke?)* slate, which are traversed by many contemporaneous veins, some composed of *Quartz*, and others of *Ferriferous*

---

* For a long period this was considered as the only Cornish habitat of this mineral; but Dr. Paris subsequently identified its presence in a sand brought from a stream near the house of Colonel Sandys at Lanarth. See " Transactions of the Royal Geological Society of Cornwall." Vol. I. p, 226.

† See a History of this curious discovery in " A Memoir on the Life and Scientific Labours of the Rev. William Gregor, by J. A. Paris, M. D."—London, 1818.

Carbonate of Lime; some small cavities are coated with fine spicular *Arragonite,* and a much rarer substance, which on a chemical examination by Mr. Gregor proved to be a *Sub-carburet of Iron,* has been found in thin plates among the laminæ of the Slate. The Reverend John Rogers has also obtained from this spot small octohedral crystals of the *Yellow Sulphuret of Copper.*

From a general review of the phenomena developed in the present excursion, Mr. Professor Sedgwick is led to conclude, that the *great Plateau of the Lizard is not composed of stratified rocks,* for although some obscure indications of an order of super-position appear near *Coverack* and *Porthalla,* yet he considers them as being too uncertain to be opposed to the clear evidence offered to the south-eastern parts of the coast, where the alternating masses of *Greenstone* and *Serpentine* so often appear, like great wedges driven side by side into the escarpment, without any arrangement whatsoever. Mr. Majendie, however, who, be it known, actually *bivouacked* in this district for a week, was satisfied that the *Greenstone* and *Serpentine* did exhibit characters of Stratification.—But we desist—feeling what no doubt our readers have likewise experienced, the dry and uninviting nature of Geological details.—Having therefore completed the task we assigned ourselves, and conducted the traveller to the more prominent and interesting objects of WESTERN CORNWALL, we take our leave. The Agriculturist, the Antiquary, the Botanist, the Geologist, and Mineralogist, must, each in his turn, have received ample gratification and instruction from his visit to this interesting and important district of the British Empire, while the Capitalist must have seen from the agriculture, the mineral treasures, the fisheries, and the commerce of the country, how many, and what great opportunities are presented for the advantageous exercise of capital; the Valetudinarian too has, as we sincerely hope, derived his share of benefit from the excursions, and felt the salutary influence of those mild and genial breezes which clothe our fields with perpetual verdure, and impart to our cottagers the enviable blessing of HEALTH and LONG LIFE.

APPENDIX.

PART I.

A DIALOGUE

Between Dr. A.— *a Physician, and Mr.* B.—
*an Invalid, on the comparative merits of dif-
ferent Climates, as places of Winter residence.*

" Ne quis *error loci* nascatur—"

Mr. B.—In a conversation which we held together
in the early part of the summer, you will remember the
promise you then gave of affording me such advice,
relative to the choice of a winter's residence, as the
declining state of my health might require. The
autumn is now rapidly advancing, and I feel that no
time should be lost in making such arrangements as
may enable me to pass the approaching winter with the
greatest prospect of benefit.

Dr. A.—I fully acquiesce in the propriety of your
resolution, and shall readily afford you any information
in my power; but you well know that to a physician

there is not a question which he approaches with so much diffidence, or dismisses with such little satisfaction.

Mr. B.—I am well aware of the difficulties to which you refer; circumstances of a moral nature, with which the physician can rarely become sufficiently acquainted, must necessarily have considerable weight in directing the decision; but in my own case it is fortunate that no such embarrassment can impede your judgment. My only object and care is the restoration of health, and my means are sufficient to enable me to pursue it in any way which may give the fairest promise of success.

Dr. A.—You mistake me, it was not to embarrassments of that kind that I was alluding.

Mr. B. — Can then any other source of difficulty exist? To a medical practitioner who is in the habit of sending his patients to all parts of Europe in search of health, the real and comparative advantages of each locality must surely be well known.

Dr. A.—Far otherwise, my dear friend; there are few subjects upon which medical men have more widely differed. It is true that we send our pulmonary suffererers to various parts of the continent, and that we receive from them a multiplicity of reports; but then they are often totally at variance with each other upon those very points which are generally considered as the least questionable; and when we attempt to reconcile this discordance, by an appeal to meteorological records, and registers of prevalent diseases, we are mortified to find that the evidence necessary for forming a safe and practical conclusion, requires a union of industry and accuracy which has not hitherto been

found to exist in a sufficient number of collateral observers. Nor must it be forgotten, that the disease,
for the cure of which the invalid is persuaded to emi-
grate, may require a very different atmosphere in its
different stages and forms ; and after all, how often does
it happen that the sufferer is not sent abroad, until every
chance of palliation has gone by.

Mr. B.—I do not hesitate to declare that such conduct, on the part of a medical adviser, is as cruel as it
is unprincipled ; my confidence however in your in-
tegrity satisfies me that you will never abandon an
unhappy sufferer to such a useless alternative ; I must
therefore request you to state your opinion, *generally*,
as to the peculiar conditions upon which you consider
the eligibility of a climate, in the cure or palliation of
pulmonary affections, to depend.

Dr. A.—This I shall do most cheerfully, especially
in conversation with one, whose philosophical pursuits
will have already instructed him in those principles,
from which our conclusions are necessarily deduced.—
Congenial warmth, and, above all, equability of temperature, are the first objects of inquiry in the theo-
retical comparison of climates ; but these cannot be
practically ascertained, in relation to their effects upon
the human body, by the thermometer ; because they
are constantly liable to be modified by causes of which
we have no other indication but that afforded by our
sensations.

Mr. B.—That is strange ;—and, so gratuitous does
the assertion appear to me, that I should be better
satisfied were you to support it by some examples.

Dr. A.—Well then, I may instance for your satisfaction, the well known influence of peculiar winds

Q

combined with moisture, and which, although they
may produce little or no variation in the thermometer
will rapidly rob the body of its heat; the north-west
winds which so commonly blow in the southern pro-
vinces of France are decidedly more mischievous to
the pulmonary invalid than the March winds that desolate the more delicate frames in our own country,
and yet the thermometer in this case affords no indication of their nature.

Mr. B.—No one who wishes to form a just estimate
of a climate, can doubt the propriety of taking the
prevalence of wind, and the degree of atmospheric
moisture into the account; although reasoning, from
analogy, I should not suppose that this latter circumstance would be prejudicial; look at the moist and
foggy atmosphere of Holland, and yet I am told that
catarrhal affections are extremely rare in that country.

Dr. A.—Moisture must make both heat and cold
more sensible; the one, by diminishing perspiration,
the other, by increasing the conducting power of the
air;* humidity therefore may be an injurious, or a
salutary condition, according to circumstances; but
you are greatly mistaken in supposing that the Dutch
owe their immunity from Catarrh to the dampness of
their climate, for it is to be imputed to the greater
equability of its temperature.

Mr. B. You no doubt place great stress upon the
advantage of an equable climate.

Dr. A. I consider equability as the most important
condition of all ; especially where the temperature ranges at about 60° of Fahrenheit. It not only diminishes
the chance of aggravating pulmonary disease by pre-

* See Paris's Pharmacologia, vol. 1, chap. " *Expectorants.*"

venting Catarrhs, but it serves to preserve a genial and regular action of the skin, to keep the balance of blood constantly on the surface, and to prevent any undue congestion of it in the lungs. Besides, it is acknowledged on all sides, that consumption is most prevalent in countries and districts which are subject to great and rapid changes of temperature, and that it is comparatively rare in those which are free from the diurnal changes and sudden transitions which so characterise that of our own island.

Mr. B. Nothing can be more convincing than such reasoning;—but tell me for what reason you consider the temperature of 60° as an essential condition under these circumstances.

Dr. A. It is evident that no climate, however equable it may be *thermometrically*, can be considered as such in a *medical* point of view, if its temperature ranges much below the degree I have mentioned; because in that case a material change must always occur whenever the invalid quits his apartment, and goes into the open air. So that I consider a cold climate must *in effect* be always regarded as a variable one.

Mr. B. But cannot this objection be obviated by suitable cloathing?

Dr. A. To a certain extent perhaps, but recollect if you please, that there is no furnishing a great coat for the lungs, to protect their structure against the diminished temperature of the air which is breathed.

Mr. B. What opinion have you formed respecting the effects of a marine atmosphere?

Dr. A. I apprehend that question cannot be fairly answered without a reference to the symptoms and circumstances of each particular case; generally speaking,

I am induced to consider the air of the sea as not hostile to diseased lungs, except perhaps in those cases in which Hectic fever is fully established; but then again cases will sometimes occur which would appear to sanction a contrary conclusion. Thus much I should say was certainly true, that in such situations you will always experience more humidity, and that when the air is cold, that cold will in consequence be more intolerable, for the reasons I have before stated. On the other hand you must be aware that a marine situation will enjoy a more equable temperature* than one similarly situated, but remote from the ocean, and as far as that goes it will have its advantages.

Mr. B. I should much like to know what the continental physicians think of this circumstance, with reference to their own climate.

Dr. A. Upon that point you may be easily satisfied by referring to Dr. Clark's work on foreign climates.† He says that the physicians on the sea coast send their consumptive patients into the interior, and those in the interior to the shores of the Mediterranean or Adriatic. From Genoa they send them into the interior, deeming the sea air injurious to them. From Naples they frequently send such invalids to Rome. From Rome, on the other hand, they send them frequently to Civitá Vecchia, on the shores of the Mediterranean; more frequently to the shores of the Adriatic, and, occasionally, even to Naples!

Mr. B. And is this account to *satisfy* me? why I am plunged deeper in doubt than ever by such testi-

---

* See page 5 of the Guide.

† Medical Notes on Climate, Diseases, &c. in France, Italy, and Switzerland, by James Clark, M.D. London 1820.

mony. No wonder that the physician should approach the subject of Climate with diffidence when he finds those best able, from experience, to appreciate its merits, so irreconcileably at variance with each other. In the next place, let me ask whether you advocate the advantages of a Sea Voyage?

Dr. A. Not unconditionally. Dr. Young has said, and I believe with much truth, that the greatest possible equability of temperature is to be obtained in a sea voyage to a warm climate; in which the variation will seldom amount to half as much as in the most favourable situation on shore, even on a small island.

Mr. B. The very condition which, of all others, you consider the most beneficial.

Dr. A. Undoubtedly, and if you can make interest with Neptune to push you forward with his trident, and persuade Æolus to slumber quietly in his caverns, lose no time in availing yourself of such advantages; but as long as the wind " bloweth where it listeth," I entreat you, my good friend, to remain on *terra firma*; depend upon it that experience will fully sanction this advice;—of the great number of patients who have been sent on such an errand, by far the greatest proportion have had the progress of their pectoral complaints rapidly accelerated during the voyage; remember the various kinds of physical injury and distress to which you must be exposed on board of ship, before you can reach a steady and warm climate, from bad weather, and different local causes which it is not necessary to enumerate;—four and twenty hours beating to windward are sufficient to counterbalance all the advantages that might be anticipated.

Mr. B. Why you must surely have been inoculated

with the prejudices of Mr. Matthews, who tells us that the fatigue and discomfort of a vessel is much the same thing as being tossed in a blanket during one half of the day, and thrown into a pigsty for the remainder.

Dr. A. I never was more serious. If the weather be bad the patient has but one alternative, he is either half suffocated with smoke or an oppressive atmosphere in the cabin, or exposed on deck to cutting winds, rain, and cold, and to an air by far too free for diseased lungs; then again sea sickness, whatever may have been said to the contrary, reduces his strength rapidly, and if damp sheets are the *bug-bears* of land travellers, damp clothes of every description are unavoidable at sea, and which in stormy weather can seldom be dried.

Mr. B. Well, you will at least allow that the motion of a ship is preferable to that of a carriage on a rough road.

Dr. A. I will not even concede this point, and were you only to read the interesting case of Dr. Currie, I am sure that you would be soon convinced of the contrary.

Mr. B. The opinion you have now expressed is sufficient; I shall not be readily induced to make the experiment of a sea voyage; suppose me then, if you please, to have been already transported across the channel on a calm day in a Steam-boat, and tell me to what part of the continent I am to direct my steps, in order to find a suitable residence for the winter months. I take it for granted that you consider the English Climate, from June to October as salutary to natives as that of any country in the world.

Dr. A. Beyond question;—but as an invalid who seeks permanent advantage from a foreign climate must be content to remain abroad for, at least, two winters, you will readily perceive that the consideration of his residence during the summer season is not entirely a subject of indifference.

Mr. B. My inclination would lead me to the south of France in preference to a more distant residence, provided the place should meet with your full concurrence.

Dr. A. The places to which English invalids have been more usually sent are Montpellier, Marseilles, Toulon, and Hieres; but I never ventured an opinion with less reserve when I declare, that I regard the very coldest parts of our own country to be less inimical to delicate lungs than the sharp and piercing air of the places which I have just mentioned. As to Montpellier, I am at a loss to understand how it could ever have obtained a reputation for its climate; and yet so universal was the belief, that its very name became, as you must well know, a characteristic epithet to places supposed to be preeminently salubrious.

Mr. B. Is it not remarkable for its clear blue sky, the very idea of which will always carry a charm with it to an Englishman?

Dr. A. Clear and brilliant enough, but the air is at the same time so sharp and biting, that every mouthful irritates the lungs, and produces excessive coughing,— and then you are, moreover, constantly assailed by one or the other of two destructive winds,—the *Bize* bringing cold, and the *Marin,* moisture.

Mr. B. And yet to this same *Bize,* of whose sharpness you so greatly complain, did the Emperor Augustus erect an altar.

Dr. A. Very true, but we are told it was an homage like that which the Indians are said to pay to the infernal deity; to avert its wrath, not to conciliate its favour.

Mr. B.   Is the locality of Marseilles less exceptionable ?

Dr. A.   By no means.   Cold winds are always injurious, but they are rendered destructive, in a tenfold proportion, when alternated with heat.   At Marseilles the dreaded *Mistral* of Provence (a north-west wind), which is often accompanied by a clear atmosphere, and a powerful sun, reigns in all its glory.   Toulon has the damning fault of Marseilles.

Mr. B.   Is Hieres exposed to the same evil ?

Dr. A.   Not in the same degree.   It has generally the credit of being much milder, and I really believe that it is justly preferred to every other place in Provence,—but it is not free from the *Mistral.*   Dr. Clark, however, tells us that about the bases of the hills, there are some sheltered spots, where the invalid might enjoy several hours in the open air on almost every dry day, but then there exists a difficulty in reaching them at those times, when they would be most useful.

Mr. B.   I see plainly, that a residence in the south of France would never realize my hopes of recovery; perhaps Nice may be more likely to afford satisfaction?

Dr. A.   Nice, as you probably know, was first brought into vogue by our celebrated countryman, Dr. Smollet, who resided there during two winters, and it has been extolled by numerous writers since that period; the northern blasts, which rage with such fury in the south of France, are averted from this favoured valley by the maritime alps.   Dr. Smollet, in speaking of its superior mildness, when compared with Provence, says, " the north-west winds blew as cold in Provence as ever I felt them on the mountains of Scotland, whereas Nice is altogether screened from them by mountains."

Mr. B. If I have been correctly informed, the neighbourhood of Nice is on many accounts preferable to the town itself.

Dr. A. The suburbs of the ' *Croix de Marbre*' have been the favourite residence of the English, and indeed on that account are not unfrequently called the ' *Faux-bourg des Anglois*'. This spot is situated immediately beyond the river *Paglion*, which, descending from its Alpine sources, washes the western extremity of the town and falls into the bay of Nice.

Mr. B. What accommodations are to be met with at Nice ?

Dr. A. I have always understood that provisions are both good and abundant ; some of my patients, however, have complained greatly of the bread as being sour and ill tasted from the leaven. As to the other accommodations, Dr. Clark says that they are also good, making allowance always for the inconveniences which, to an English family, are inseparable from foreign houses, such as smoky apartments, ill provided fire places, &c.

Mr. B. Now state, if you please, the objections that may be urged against Nice.

Dr. A. In the commencement of the winter, this valley is remarkably infested with mosquitoes, which greatly annoy strangers, especially children. During the months of November, December, and January, the climate would seem to embrace all the qualities so favourable to pectoral complaints, but the three following months are by no means unexceptionable. Although Nice be protected from the *Mistral*, yet in the spring of the year it is infested with cold sharp winds from the

east, and north and south-east, which are highly mischievous to the valetudinarian.

Mr. B. It is clear then that he should quit Nice at
this season.

Dr. A. That is not so easy as you may suppose, for
unless he leaves it by sea, he must not venture to depart
by any of the usual roads before the month of May; for
should he direct his route to Turin, he will have a very
rough and hazardous journey over the " *Col de Tende*,"
and may perchance be caught in a snow storm; if on
the other hand, he returns by France, he must cross the
" *Estrelles*," and expose himself to the cold winds of
Provence.

Mr. B. Well these are strong objections; but taking
into consideration all the advantages and disadvantages
of Nice, will not the former so greatly preponderate,
as to entitle it to the character it has long enjoyed as
an eligible *winter* residence for the consumptive?

Dr. A. I fear that medical experience will not
sanction such a conclusion. Catarrhal affections are
frequent amongst the inhabitants, and it has been remarked by those best able to investigate the subject,
that the progress of pulmonary disease is rather accelerated than retarded by this climate. If you will allow
me, I will read a passage from a late work by Dr.
Carter, which places this subject in a very striking
point of view. " Notwithstanding the mildness of
Nice, it appeared to be of little or no service to persons labouring under confirmed consumption; during
the winter I was there, I saw no instance of great
amendment, and I even doubted whether life was not
shortened in some instances by a residence there. Some
medical men were clearly of that opinion; and as their

interest should have led them to speak well of Nice, they must have been pretty strongly impressed with the conviction of its climate being hurtful to people in con- firmed Phthisis, before they could have been induced to make this opinion public." *

Mr. B. This is discouraging; but is the testimony of Dr. Carter supported by other authorities?

Dr. A. By many others. Here is a work by Dr. Clark, who is himself resident at Rome, and a physician of great intelligence ; he not only confirms the opinion of Dr. Carter, but adduces that of Professor Foderé who practised at Nice for more than six years, and who in a conversation with Dr. Clark, made the following strong observation. " There is one thing certain, Sir, you may safely assure your countrymen, that it is a very bad practice to send their consumptive patients to Nice." M. Foderé moreover observed, that consumption in this district is not, as in Switzerland, on the banks of the Soane, and in Alsace, a chronic disease; but, on the contrary, he has often seen it terminate in forty days; he says that the physician of the countries just men- tioned would be quite astonished at the quickness with which one attack of pulmonary hemorrhage succeeds another, how readily the tubercles suppurate, and how speedily the lungs are destroyed." He is even inclined to believe that there exists, on the shores of the Medi- terranean, some source of evil not appreciable by meteorological observations.

---

* A Short Accouut of some of the Principal Hospitals of France, Italy, Switzerland, and the Netherlands, with Remarks upon the Climate and Diseases ef those Countries. By H. W. Carter, M.D. London 1819.

Mr. B. Enough of Nice. What of Pisa?

Dr. A. You may perhaps remember that Mr. Matthews, in his comparison of these two places, says,
" I believe that Pisa is the very best place on the continent during the winter for complaints of the chest ;
and Nice, of which I speak from good authority, is
perhaps the very worst. The air of the first, which is
situated in a low plain, is warm, mild, and muggy ;
that of the second is pure, keen, and piercing."

Mr. B. To speak honestly, I entertain a very high
respect for Mr. Matthews as an intelligent and agree-
able tourist, but he is the very last authority upon
which I could repose my confidence, with regard to the
salubrity of a climate ; his observations upon this head
are too fretful and petulant to afford satisfaction.

Dr. A. His remarks upon Nice and Pisa will certainly justify the opinion you have formed ; for there
does not exist such a striking difference in the climate
of these places as he has been induced to believe ; although the latter town is certainly milder than Nice,
and possesses the advantage of having good roads leading to it from all parts of Italy, so that the invalid may
leave it with safety much earlier than he could Nice.

Mr. B. Are the spring winds less violent than at
Nice?

Dr. A. Scarcely. The site of the houses, however,
is better calculated to defend you from their influence.
On the northern bank of the Arno, there is a crescent
which faces the south, and is well protected from the
north winds ; this situation ought always to be selected
by invalids who winter at Pisa.

Mr. B. If I resolve to winter in Italy, I shall probably prefer Pisa. I confess that I have received a

prejudice against Rome, as well as Naples, from the reports of some friends who have lately returned from those places; but I should be glad to hear your opinion upon the subject.

Dr. A. Rome and Naples ought not to be named in the same breath, unless indeed for the sake of contrast. Rome possesses many points of excellence as a winter residence, but as to Naples at this season, I would not recommend an invalid, on any account, to try its climate :—conceive the effects of a hot sun with a winter wind of piercing bitterness ! " *Vedi Napoli e po' mori,*" says the proverb, and no wonder that it has received so many illustrations from the English. Upon this one point at least we must all concur with Mr. Matthews: " If," says he, " a man be tired of the slow lingering progress of consumption, let him repair to Naples; and, the *denouement* will be much more rapid."

Mr. B. But what of Rome—of the Eternal City ?

Dr. A. That vehemence of expression, my good friend, betrays your polarity ; in spite of your avowal I see clearly that your wishes point to the ancient Mistress of the world.

Mr. B. You really mistake me ;—depend upon it that I shall undertake no pilgrimage but to the temple of Hygeia.

Dr. A. Rome has, by far, too many temptations for the invalid, and I confess that from the accounts which I have received from my patients, I am unable to discover any advantages equivalent to the risks.

Mr. B. I am even told that the climate of Rome is much colder than that of Nice in the winter.

Dr. A. You have been rightly informed ; in addition to which, the streets are damp and chilly, and so variable in temperature, that there is not unfrequently a difference of twenty degrees between one street and another.

Mr. B. In what then does its excellence consist?

Dr. A. It is decidedly the best spring residence in Italy. The air is much more moist than that of Nice; and, at this season, it has the advantage of being less liable to cold winds; although it must be confessed that the *Tramontana* (a sharp northerly wind,) is sometimes felt with considerable severity, but it does not affect the human body like the dry cold winds of Provence.

Mr. B. The prejudice which exists in my mind against Rome has arisen from the circumstance of many of my friends having suffered severely from head-ache, during their residence there.

Dr. A. Upon that point, I fear my opinion will rather strengthen than remove your prejudice. I have no hesitation in stating, that the same complaint has been frequently made to me; and even Dr. Clark, the English resident physician, confirms the objection.*

Mr. B. And then comes the frightful *Malaria*.

Dr. A. The stranger has nothing to fear from these exhalations between October and the middle of May,

---

* " There is one class of affections for which the Atmosphere of Rome appeared to me unfavourable. These are head-aches arising from a tendency to a fullness about the head. In many cases among the English residents, I found persons not previously subject to head-aches affected with them here, and some already liable to them had been aggravated. Apoplexy, I was told, was at one time so frequent at Rome that a day of public fasting was ordered, and a particular form of prayer addressed to St. Anthony to avert so dreadful a calamity from the Holy city."

after which period I should not recommend any invalid to protract his visit.

Mr. B. But suppose his object is to remain two winters at Rome,—where is he to find refuge during these intervals ?

Dr. A. In the vicinity of Rome there are many spots which will furnish a very eligible residence during the hot weather, such are Albano, Frascati, Tivoli, Castel Gandolfo.

Mr. B. After what you have said, I think it is scarcely worth while for an invalid to encounter the fatigues of so long a journey ; but you have not yet mentioned Florence.

Dr. A. Its climate is almost as changeable as our own, and far more mischievous, as its Siberian winds alternate with a temperature equal to that of our finest days in spring. The summer, however, is delightful, the heat being greatly tempered by the Apennines. Bicchierai, an Italian Physician of eminence, used to say, that he wondered how any body could *live* at Florence in the winter, or *die* there in the summer.

Mr. B. Upon the whole you have presented me with a very discouraging view of the Italian Climate ; and I have always understood that Lisbon is intolerable to an Englishman from its filth.

Dr. A. Lisbon is out of the question : the character of its climate may be summed up in a few words. Its winter temperature is neither mild nor equable, and its spring is remarkable for dense and cold fogs ; and as to what an Englishman calls comfort, there is not a city in the world where it is so systematically neglected.

Mr. B. Suppose I wave the objections to a sea voyage and set sail for Sicily ?

Dr. A. In that case you will undoubtedly find a fine climate, superior in most respects to that of the Italian continent. The winter and spring seasons are remarkably mild, provided you select Palermo for your residence; Messina is exposed to cold piercing easterly winds from the mountains of Calabria.

Mr. B. I have heard Catania well spoken of.

Dr. A. Its atmosphere is too sulphureous; in addition to which every egress from the town is difficult and unpleasant, owing to the lava from the Volcano. But there is in my opinion an insuperable objection to the Sicilian climate from the extreme heat of its summer, from which the invalid cannot easily escape.

Mr. B. Well then, Malta.

Dr. A. Dr. Domeier, in his account of this climate, tells us that the thermometer seldom varies in this island more than 6° in the twenty-four hours, or stands below 51°, even in the depth of winter: but then the summer, which is protracted even to the month of November, is extremely mischievous from its heat, the force of which is severely felt in a country where there is scarcely any visible foliage, the place of hedges being universally occupied by stone walls.

Mr. B. Let me hear what you have to say with respect to the other islands which have gained celebrity for their climates, such as Madeira, the Bermudas, Jamaica,—

Dr. A. You must be well aware that these places are, generally speaking, beyond the reach of the ordinary class of English invalids. Madeira has been greatly extolled by Dr. Adams, who even ventures to assert that in cases of consumption, if the patient does not saunter away his time, after his physician has ad-

vised him to quit England, we may with certainty promise him a cure. In the West Indies it is agreed by
all authors, that consumptive affections are almost unknown, and that scrofula in all its forms is uncommon.

Mr. B. Would you recommend a residence in the
West Indies to a person who has free control over his
movements?

Dr. A. If we may be allowed to draw any inference
from the qualities of a climate, as indicated by the thermometer, or by its effects on the constitution of the
inhabitants, there can be but little doubt that a residence in the Bermudas, in a temperate and sheltered
part of Jamaica, or in some other of the West India
Islands, would present every advantage, towards the
recovery of a consumptive patient, that climate alone
can bestow.

Mr. B. I thank you sincerely, my good Sir, for the
patience and candour with which you have discussed the
subject of climate. I am fully sensible of the difficulties
with which it is encompassed, and of the utter impos-
sibility of expecting from medical advice a satisfactory
solution of the many problems which it involves. Every
invalid must, to a certain extent, rely upon his own
judgment; but before I finally decide upon the place
of my destination, allow me to trespass still farther upon your patience, in order to learn whether, after all,
there be not some favoured spot in our own country,
where I might seek shelter from the approaching
season, and which would supersede the necessity of
travelling to a foreign land?

Dr. A. I should say to a person, who had been
accustomed to the colder and more exposed parts of our
island, try the effects of some more genial situation;

and such a change would be as likely to favour convalescence as an emigration to the continent; for although by such a step, he might not obtain an equally
favourable atmosphere, he would more than counterbalance the difference by ensuring the advantages of
English comforts.

Mr. B. And to what parts of England would you
direct him?

Dr. A. There are particular spots on the coast of
Hampshire and Sussex which have been long considered
as eligible places of winter residence; such are South-
ampton and Hastings, which are certainly less subject
to the effect of the Northern and Eastern winds than
many parts of our island; but they are not to be put in
competition with Sidmouth, Dawlish, or Torquay in
Devonshire, and still less with Penzance in Cornwall,
which, after all, is the only situation which can be
fairly said to possess any very material advantages from
the mildness of its winter. I speak this from well
grounded observation and experience. The Climate of
Penzance is unlike that of any other part of the island.

Mr. B. I remember having received a favourable
impression with respect to the climate of that place,
from the perusal of a small work, entitled, a Guide to
the Mount's Bay and the Land's End; a copy was lent
me by Sir ⸺ ⸺, and I have since endeavoured to
purchase one, but find that it is out of print.

Dr. A. Are you not aware then that you have been
conversing with its author?—The book has been for
some time out of print, but a second edition is nearly
ready for publication; and, with your permission, I
shall introduce, as nearly as my memory will serve,

the conversation which we have just held together upon the subject of Climate.

Mr. B. By all means ;—the questions which I have submitted for your opinion, are such as must naturally suggest themselves to every invalid who is in search of a winter residence, and as your little work, as far as I recollect, is intended for the same class of persons, its practical utility will be materially enhanced by the addition you have just proposed.

APPENDIX.—PART II.

An Account of the First Celebration of the
KNILLIAN GAMES at St. IVES.

Alluded to at page 158 of this work.

WE trust that our readers will find some amusement
and relaxation, after the fatigue of their day's excursion,
in the following *Jeu d'Esprit*, as originally written by
an eye witness of the festivity ; an institution which,
adds the said writer, will go far to preserve the tone of
the Cornish character, and which can never be neglected while the Cornish men continue to be brave, and
the Cornish women to be virtuous.

The celebration of the Games at Olympia, after the
revolution of every four years, formed the chief date of
time among the Greeks; and perhaps in future the inhabitants of the West of England will reckon the years,
as they pass, by the quinquennial return of the games
at St. Ives.

I ought rather to have begun by stating, that John
Knill, Esq. a gentleman formerly of great eminence in
the above mentioned town, has bequeathed the income
of a considerable estate to be distributed by the trustees
in a variety of prizes to those who may excel in racing,
in rowing, and in wrestling. A large sum is to be
divided among a band of virgins, who are to be dressed
all in white, and with four matrons, and a company of
musicians preceding them, are to walk in pairs to the
summit of the hill, which is near the town of St. Ives,

where they are to dance and chaunt a hymn round the far famed mausoleum.

Ten guineas are appointed to be expended in a dinner at the grand hotel in the town, of which six of the principal inhabitants are to partake ; and this festival is to be repeated every fifth year for ever.

From the earliest periods of history, the Cornish have been famous for their enthusiastic fondness of the athletic exercises of hurling, racing, wrestling, and rowing, and for the pious fervour of the hymns which the Druids instructed them to sing round the Cromlechs of the departed brave.

By establishing rewards for superiority in amusements in which the Cornish still delight to excel, Mr. Knill has shewn the patriotic feelings of his local attachments ; while by the appropriate selection of the spot where these pastimes are to take place, he has given ample proof of the correctness of his taste. The enormous statue of Jupiter at Elis pointed out that part of Peloponnesus to the taste of the Greeks, as the most proper place for the celebration of the Olympic Games; and a sympathy of feeling and sentiment induced Mr. Knill to order that the Mausoleum, which he erected in the year 1782 should be the centre of the quinquennial festivities. This proud pyramid, whose base is situated on the summit of a rock, and whose apex is often concealed among the clouds, has hitherto formed only an object of ornamental magnificence, or a guide to the tempest tost mariner ; but henceforth it will be regarded as the monument of fame—the pillar of the west—the Cornish column !

Monday last was the day appointed for the first celebration. I was present at the scene, and am induced to think, from this first specimen, that the rites of the hill will be celebrated in succeeding years with increased fervour and renewed admiration. Weak as my powers of description are, your readers may, perhaps, from the following account, conceive some idea of the interesting spectacle.

Early in the morning the roads from Helston, from Truro, and from Penzance, were lined with horses and vehicles of every description. These were seen amidst clouds of dust, pouring down the sides of the adjacent mountains ; while thousands of travellers on foot chose the more pleasant route through the winding passages of the vallies. At noon the assembly was formed. The wrestlers entered the ring ;—the troop of virgins dressed, all in white, advanced with solemn step, which was regulated by the notes of harmony. The spectators ranged themselves along the sides of the hills which inclose the extensive bay, while the pyramid on the summit seemed pointing to the sun, who appeared in all the majesty of light, rejoicing at the scene.

At length the Mayor of Saint Ives appeared in his robes of state. The signal was given. The flags were displayed in waving splendour from the towers of the castle. Here the wrestlers exerted their sinewy strength ; there the rowers, in their various dresses of blue, white, and red, urged the gilded prows of their boats through the sparkling waves of the ocean ; while the hills echoed to the mingled shouts of the victors, the dashing of the oars, the songs of the virgins, and the repeated plaudits of the admiring crowd, who stood so thick upon the crescent, which is formed by the surrounding mountains, as to appear, if I may so express myself, *one living amphitheatre.*

The ladies and gentlemen of Penzance returned to an elegant dinner which they had ordered to be prepared at the Union Hotel ; and a splendid ball concluded the entertainment of the evening. The jolly god presided, —but a reproving smile from Venus restrained him, if he ventured beyond the due bounds of decorum. Hilarity and beauty danced to the most delicious notes of harmony ; till the rosy finger of Aurora pointed to the hour at which the quinquennial festivities should close. Perhaps to many the visions of the night brought back the joys of the day, and the feet danced, the heart throbbed, and the cheek glowed, when the eye-lids were closed in sleep.

A SONG,

Written by one of the Head Poets of London for Mr. KNILL's GAMES at Saint Ives.

(To the tune of " *Boys and Girls come out to play.*")

Sung at the Mausoleum, by a Minstrel adorned with Ribbons.

KNILL commands, and all obey,
Lads and Lasses haste away,
Aunts and Uncles,* Maids and Wives,
All are gay, at gay St. Ives.
    No tongue is mute or foot is still,
    But *One and All*† are on the hill,
    In chorus round the tomb of Knill.

This you surely may rely on,
Paul, Penzance, nor Marazion,
Never saw in all their lives
Such sport as now is at St. Ives.
    No tongue, &c.

---

* *Aunts and Uncles.* A Cornish epithet indiscriminately applied to elderly persons.
    † *One and All* is the Cornish motto.

Some in gigs and coaches flocking,
Some without or shirt or stocking,
All are crowding---not a hack
But has three upon his back.
  No tongue, &c.

Of Virgins pure---(let envy squint,
And malice sneer, there's nothing in't)
Of Virgins pure a throng advance,
And round the tomb in circles dance,
  No tongue, &c.

Boys on gingerbread are feeding,
Cudgel-broken pates are bleeding;
Races running, Wrestlers falling,
Bones are cracking, women squalling.
  No tongue, &c.

Thro' the breaking wave below,
Rowers urge the bounding prow;
While many a Tub and many a Ray ‡
Sport around in finny play.
  No tongue, &c.

All are running---what's the matter?
Why, to see the fine Regatta.
Earth and water, hill and bay,
Share the frolic of the day.
  No tongue, &c.

Oh! it glads the heart to see e'm
Gamble round the Mausoleum.
All is joy : and laughter shakes
All the merry land of Hakes.†
  No tongue, &c.

---

‡ Common fish at St. Ives.
† St. Ives abounds with a fish called a *Hake.*

What a pother ! what a deal is
Talk'd about the games at Elis :
Such as they---no not a million
Equal what we call the Knillian.
      No tongue, &c.

Knill commands, and all obey,
Lads and lasses haste away,
All the world and all his wives.
What was Greece to gay St. Ives ! !
    No tongue is mute, no foot is still,
    But *One and All* are on the hill
    In chorus round the tomb of Knill.

An appropriate Chorus to be sung round the Tomb by the
Virgins.

    Quit the bustle of the Bay,
    Hasten, Virgins, come away ;
    Hasten to the mountain's brow,
    Leave, oh ! leave St. Ives below !
    Haste to breathe a purer air
    Virgins fair, and pure as fair.
    Quit St. Ives and all her treasures,
    Fly her soft voluptuous pleasures,
    Fly her sons and all the wiles,
    Lurking in their wanton smiles ;
    Fly her splendid midnight halls,
    Fly the revels of her Balls ;
    Fly, oh ! fly the chosen seat,
    Where vanity and fashion meet.
    Hither hasten ; form the ring,
    Round the tomb in chorus sing,
    And on the lofty mountain's brow
        Aptly dite,
    (Just as we should be, all in white)
    Leave all our *Cowels*,* and our cares below.

------

* See the explanation of this term at page 34.

A CORNISH DIALOGUE

Between GRACE PENVEAR and MARY TREVISKEY.

—

GREACEY.

Fath and Trath than! I bleeve in ten Parishes round
Sichey Roag, sichey Vellan es nat to ba found.

MALLY.

Whoats' tha' fussing, Un Greacey! long wetha Cheel Vean?

GREACEY.

A fussing a ketha! oads splet 'es ould breane!
Our Martn's cum'd hum cheeld so drunk as a beast,
And so cross as the Gallish from Perran-zan feaast:
A cum'd in a tottering, cussing, and sweering
So hard as a Stompses, and tarving and teering!

MALLY.

Naver meynd et un Greacey, goa, poat en to bed
Al sleep ale tha lecker aweay froam es head.

GREACEY.

I'd nat goa a neest en to fang tha Kings Crown,
For a sweers ef I speek to'an al cleev ma skuel down:
Tha navar en ale tha boarn daeys, fath and shoar,
Dedst behould sichey Maze-gerry Pattick a foar.

(Fuss) [a low cant word] a tumult, a bustle. Swift.
(Un) Aunt—a title usually given to an elderly woman.
(Vean) Cornish for little] Cheel Vean—little Child.
(Tarving) [a cant word] struggling, convulsions, *Tarvings.*
(Fang) [Saxon] to gripe, receive, &c. Shakespear.
(Maze-gerry Pattick) a mad brutish or frolicsome fool.

Why, a scat ale to Midjans and Jowds for the noans,
A clom Buzza of scale melk about on tha scoans.
And a raak'd up a showl for to steeve ma' outright,
But I'm run'd awaey, readdy to feyntey for freyt!
Loard! tell ma un Mally! whaat shall Ey do by 'an?
For Zoundtikins Deth! Ey'm a fear'd to cum ny'an.

MALLY.

I know whoat Ey'd gee'an ef so bee 'twor my case,
Ey'd scat tha ould Chacks aa'n; Ey'd trem 'an un Greace.

GREACEY.

Ey'm afeard o'my leyf to coam ny tha ould Vellan,
Else pleas faather! Ey bleeve Ey shu'd murely kill 'an.
Wor ever poor creychar so baal'd and aboos'd,
Ma heep here leyke bazzom, tha Roag have a bruis'd.
Ey mad for 'es sopar a Muggety Pye,
But a shaan't clunk a croom a'te Ey wish Ey meay die!

MALLY.

Aye! Ey tould tha afore that tha jobb wor a done,
That tha'd'st find out tha odds 'ate, so shoor as a gun;
But tha' wouds'nt hark to ma for doubting, for why
That beshoor, that tha knowd'st 'en mooch better than Ey;
But Ey knaw'd tha good trem 'ane befour tha's't a got 'en;
Ey cou'd tell tha a mashes of stoareys about en;
But tha' aanserds't soa heytish and shrinkt up tha noaz:
'A gissing 'twor greeat stromming leys Ey sopoaz!
But there's one of es praenks Ey shall aleweays remembar
'Twill be three years agone coam tha eighth of Novembar,

(Midjans and Jouds) shreds and tatters.
(Noans) [Nonce] on purpose.
(Clom Buzza) a coarse earthen pot.
(Scoans) the pavement. (Showl) a shovel. (Steeve) stave.
(Scat) to give a blow, to break. (Chacks) cheeks.
(Murely) almost. (Baal'd) mischievously beaten.
(Bazzom) of a blue or purple colour.
(Muggety Pye) a pye made of sheeps guts, parsley and cream,
pepper and salt. (Clunk) swallow. (Croom) crumb,
(Mashes) a great many, nnmber, &c.

Ey'd two pretty young Mabjers as eyes cu'd behould,
So fat as tha Botar; jest iteen wiks ould,
Tha wor picking about in tha Tewn plaace for meat,
Soa Ey hev downe sum Pillas amongst mun to eat:
When who but your man comd a tott'ring along
Soa drunk, that Ey thoft fath, ad fale in tha dung!
'A left tomble 'es Hoggan-bag jest by tha doar,
Soa I caled to tha man as one wud to be shoor,
Şez Ey, Martyn! dust hire Cheeld! teak up tha bag,
" Arrea" sez a, " for whoat beest a caleing me Dog?"
And dreev'd forth toweards ma, nar bettar nar wuss
Nack'd the Mabjers boath steff, we a gaert mawr o' fuss;
Ley'k enow ef Ey hadnt shov'd haastis awaey
A'd a done as a ded to Jan Rous t'oather daey,
When a gote en eis tantrums, a wilfull ould Devel,
A slam'd tha poor Soal on tha head we a Yevel;
Fath and Soal than un Gracey ef so bee a doent aelter
Ey bleev e ma conshance el swing en a haelter.

GREACEY.

When tha Leker es runn'd awaey every drap
'Tis too late to ba thenking of plugging the Tap,
And marridge must goa as the Loard do ordean,
But a Passon wud swear to ba used so Cheeld Vean.
Had Ey smilt out tha coose 'ane but neyne weeks ago
Ey'd never a had tha ould Vellan Ey know,

(Mabjers) Mab Hens—young fowls two-thirds grown.

(Pillas) [Pilez—Cornish] the *avena nuda* or naked oats of Ray;
bald, bare or naked oats without husks.

(Hoggan) Hogan in Cornish British signifies a Hawthorn berry;
also any thing mean or vile; but here it means a Pork pasty; and
now indeed a Tinner's Pasty is called *a Hoggan.*

(Arrea) Arria [vulg. for Ria] O strange.

(Gaert) great, " gaert mawr o Fuss," great root of Furze.

(Haestis) hastily. (Yevil) a Dung fork with three prongs.

(Passon) Parson. (Coose) course or way of him.

(Neyne weeks)—as though they had been married but nine
weeks, whereas in the third line, she is addressed by Un Mally as

But a vowd and a swear'd that if Ey'd by hes weyf
That Ey naver shud lack ale tha daeys o' ma leyf;
And a broft me a Nakin and Corn saave from Preen;
En ma conshance thoft Ey, Ey shall leve leyk a Queen.
But 'tes plaguey provoking, od rat es ould head!
To be pooted and flopt soa! Ey wish a war dead.
Why a spent haafe es fangings laast Saterday neyt,
Leyk enow by this teym 'tes gone every dyte.
But Ey'll tame tha ould Devel, afor et es long,
Ef Ey caant we ma Viestes—Ey will we ma Tongue.

' long wetha Cheeld vean.' This will be readily explained by
noticing a custom very prevalent among the lower ranks of the
county, as will appear by the following anecdote. A friend of mine
who was one year an officer in one of the mining parishes, told me
that of fifty-five couples married during that year, it was *manifest*
by the appearance of fifty of the ladies, that they ought to have
been married several moons before. A young man, to the honor
of the county be it said, (even if the practice be to its disparage-
ment) needs no compulsion to marry his lass when in this condition.

(Nackin) Handkerchief. (Preen) Penryn. (Pooted) kicked.
(Fangings) gettings or wages. (Viestes) Fists.

CARN BREH,†

AN ODE HITHERTO UNPUBLISHED,

By Dr. WALCOT,

BETTER KNOWN BY THE POETICAL APPELLATION OF

PETER PINDAR.*

While nature slumbers in the shade,
  And Cynthia, cloth'd in paly light,
Walks her lone way, the mount I tread,
  Majestic mid the gloom of night.
With reverence to the lofty hill I bow,
Where Wisdom, Virtue, taught their founts to flow.

Wan, on yon rocks' aspiring steep
  Behold a Druid form, forlorn!
I see the white rob'd phantom weep—
  I hear to heaven his wild harp mourn.
The temples open'd to the vulgar eye;
And Oaks departed, wake his inmost sigh.

---

† For a description of this hill see page 208.

* Dr. Walcot was apprenticed to his uncle, who was an apothecary at Fowey in Cornwall, and after having practised for some years in the West Indies, he settled as a Physician at Truro: after residing there for some time, he suddenly quitted the county, in consequence of a law suit in which he was engaged against the Corporation of Truro; the dispute related to the right of their putting upon him a parish apprentice; when he sold his effects, shut up his house, and informed the officers that if they were determined to carry their point, they might put the apprentice into the empty building, as he should never enter it again.

O ! lover of the twilight hour,
   That calls thee from the tombs of death,
To haunt the cave, the time-struck tower,
   The sea-girt cliff, the stormy heath ;
Sweet is thy minstrelsy to him whose lays
First sung this hallow'd hill of ancient days.

   Yet not this Druid-scene alone
      Inspires the gloom-delighted muse ;
   Ah ! many a hill to fame unknown,
      With awe the tuneful wanderer views ;
And oft while midnight lends her list'ning ear,
Sings darkling, to the solitary sphere.

   Poor Ghost ! no more the Druid band
      Shall watch, Devotion-wrapt, their fire,
   No more, high sounding thro' the land,
      To Virtue strike the plauding lyre.
The snake along the frowning fragment creeps,
And fox obscene beneath the shadow sleeps.

   No more beneath the golden hook
      The treasures of the grove shall fall ;
   Time triumphs o'er each vanish'd oak—
      The power whose might shall crush this ball—
Yet, yet, till Nature droops the head to die
Compassion grant each monument a sigh.

   The bards, in lays sublime, no more
      The warrior's glorious deeds relate ;
   Whose patriot arm a thunder bore,
      That hurl'd his country's foe to fate :
Lo ! mute the harp near each pale Druid hung,
Mute, like the voice that once accordant sung.

Save when the wandering breeze of morn,
  Or eve's wild gale with wanton wing,
To hear the note of sorrow mourn,
  Steals to the silent sleeping string,
And wildly brushing, wakes with sweetest swell,
The plaintive trembling spirit of the shell.

Here Virtue's awful voice was heard,
  That pour'd the instructive truth profound,
Here Cornwall's sons that voice rever'd,
  Where sullen silence sleeps around.
See where she sung, sad, melancholy, tread,
A pensive pilgrim o'er th' unconscious dead.

She calls on Alda's, Odred's name,
  Sons to the darken'd world of yore !
Lur'd by whose eagle-pinion'd fame,
  The stranger left his native shore,
Daring, his white sail to the winds he gave,
And sought fair knowledge o'er the distant wave.

Tho' few these awful rocks revere,
  And temples that deserted lie,
The muse shall ask the tenderest tear
  That ever dropt from Pity's eye,
T' embalm the ruins that her sighs deplore,
Where Wisdom, Virtue dwelt, but dwell no more.

London : printed by William Phillips,
George Yard, Lombard Street.

For EU product safety concerns, contact us at Calle de José Abascal, 56–1°, 28003 Madrid, Spain or eugpsr@cambridge.org.

www.ingramcontent.com/pod-product-compliance
Ingram Content Group UK Ltd.
Pitfield, Milton Keynes, MK11 3LW, UK
UKHW010347140625
459647UK00010B/899